END

G000123706

"Christians are united in confidence that the l...
This is the great hope for which the church mu...
When? Dr. Bill Anderson brings his keen theo...
dous importance for the church. This book is a...
and pastoral application. Bill Anderson is to be...
this important book. Even those who disagree w... ... ...conclusion will be stretched and edified by a serious confrontation with the evidence and arguments he presents. I can only wish that every pastor would be so careful and thoughtful in declaring and teaching the truth of our Blessed Hope."

— R. Albert Mohler, Jr.
President, Southern Baptist Theological Seminary

"Anyone interested in the biblical account of the Lord's return—and all Christians should be—here is the best, most convincing, and exhaustive treatment of this subject I have ever read. It presents the Second Coming of Christ in a definite scriptural pattern and undergirds it all from a historical, theological perspective. I most highly recommend this work to all who "look for His coming."

— Dr. Lewis A. Drummond
Chancellor of Schools of Evangelism
The Cove, Billy Graham Training Center

"One of the best responses to the Scriptures used by the pre-tribulation rapturists and their objections to the post-tribulation position that I have seen for many years. The spirit, tone, fairness, and scholarship exhibited by Dr. Anderson all facilitate the interesting readability of this book. Anyone interested in a thorough study of the timing of the Rapture should possess this book. Moreover, no serious student seeking a biblical eschatology should be without this book. It is one of the most significant contributions to the field of pre-millennial eschatology in print today. A must read for all prophecy lovers and for those who want to be adequately prepared for future prophetic events."

— Dr. Bill Crews
Host of international telecast "Awakening Hour"

"Dr. Anderson has done Christians a real service in the publication of this book. In a day when the dispensational, pretribulational view of end-time events has been so widely publicized as the only Biblical view, it is refreshing to see the historic views of the Christian church expounded in popular style. I hope that the book will be widely distributed and widely read."

—William E. Bell, Jr., Ph.D.
Senior Professor, Biblical Studies
Dallas Baptist University

"Left behind? You're already left behind if you don't have a copy of Dr. Bill Anderson's Rapture? Sure...but When?, the prophecy book that's miles ahead of others. So, catch up!"

— Dave MacPherson
Author of The Rapture Plot

RAPTURE??

Sure... *but when?*

What if the end isn't really as so many have portrayed it?

WILLIAM E. ANDERSON

GREEN KEY BOOKS

RAPTURE? SURE...*BUT WHEN?*
William E. Anderson
Published by Green Key Books

©2003 by William E. Anderson. All Rights Reserved.
International Standard Book Number: 0970599684

ALL RIGHTS RESERVED

No part of this publication may be reproduced, stored in a retrieval system, or transmitted in any form or by any means—electronic, mechanical, photocopying, recording, or otherwise—without prior written permission.

Scripture quotations, unless otherwise noted, are taken from HOLY BIBLE, KING JAMES VERSION. Public Domain.

For information:
GREEN KEY BOOKS
2514 ALOHA PLACE
HOLIDAY, FLORIDA 34691

Library of Congress Cataloging-in-Publication Data available upon request.

Printed in the United States of America
04 05 06 7 5 4 3 2

Acknowledgements

Rapture...has been a labor of love for God's Word and work in the earth and for all who love both. As all authors learn, however, the emphasis might well be put on the word *labor*!

I am indebted to all who encouraged me to write, particularly Dave MacPherson and Dr. William E. Bell, both masters of the subject they nudged a true neophyte to address.

I express appreciation, too, to Peter Castor, president of Green Key Books, for all his invaluable assistance and, especially, to his wife and acquisitions editor at Green Key, Krissi Castor, who saw the book through, with amazing patience, from conception to birth—even as she was preparing for another birth, that of her daughter, Mackenzie Faith.

I dedicate this book, with genuine affection, to two groups of five, that of my family: Addie, my wife, and our four children, Mark, Karen, Gaye, and Hazel; and the five churches which I pastored—Central Baptist Church, Ingleside; Lorena Baptist Church, Lorena; First Baptist Church, McGregor; First Baptist Church, Euless, all of Texas; and Calvary Baptist Church in Clearwater, Florida.

William E. Anderson
Clearwater, Florida

Table of Contents

Introduction

Before embarking on another expedition into the study of biblical apocalyptic writings, it seems appropriate to ask the questions: Why even study prophecy? Isn't prophecy too difficult for the average Christian to understand anyway? And aren't there so many competing, seemingly far-fetched theories out there that perceptive people should acknowledge such and bid the whole enterprise goodbye? And is it really possible to come to any solid conclusions about biblical predictions regarding the future? What makes any author, including the author of this book, an authority on the subject? And besides, can't a committed Christian get along without prophecy anyway? Really, what good does such study accomplish?

Good questions. And understandable. However, the answer is that every Christian should study prophecy because:

1. Approximately one-fourth of the entire Bible is comprised of predictive prophecy at the time of writing. It could not be a wise thing to allow one-fourth of God's book to exist unread and unheeded.

2. As Christians, we are able to understand and withstand the onslaught of historical events if only we are familiar with prophecy. A horrific time of tribulation, the likes of which the world has never seen, will one day fall upon the earth. How can people—whoever populates the earth in those days—face such times redemptively without knowing something about the biblical predictions regarding those dark days? In addition, the study of Bible prophecy helps us interpret events for the wider secularized, pagan culture. How can inhabitants of such a culture understand the meaning of end-times events if Christians don't tell

them what God has promised will come to pass? Without the input of Christians, the secular mind, no matter how astute, can never understand the meaning of history.

3. Predictive prophecy, it could be cogently argued, is the most powerful demonstration of the Bible's inspiration. It is a phenomenon unique to the Bible. No other religion is truly predictive in the biblical sense. It does no good to argue that, say, a Nostradamas or a Jeane Dixon or an Edgar Cayce predicted some things which came to pass. Such "prophecies" are altogether of a different order than biblical prophecy, and besides, even a stopped clock is right twice a day. The biblical rule of true prophecy is this: *every detail must come true, or it is not genuine prophecy.*

    Further, when the specific prophecy does come true against astronomical odds (such as, for instance, the promised rebirth of the nation Israel, which occurred after 2500 years of the Jews being dispersed among the nations), that amounts to a compelling demonstration of the Bible's veracity.

4. All Christians draw daily strength from the promises of the prophetic Scriptures, whether they realize it or not. Such events as our own resurrection (or rapture), the (attendant) return of Christ, the forgiveness of sins, the promise of Heaven, eternal fellowship with the redeemed of all the ages, and God's providential care in the meantime are all among God's prophetic promises—truths which give Christians joy, strength, meaning, and purpose on a daily basis.

5. Christians are explicitly promised a blessing upon the student of prophecy. God told John the Revelator, "Blessed *is* he who reads and those who hear the words of this prophecy, *and keep those things which are written in it.*" (Revelation 1:3, author's italics) This passage also gives witness to the moral power of prophecy; that is, it refers to the holy living which prophecy inspires.

6. God is pleased when Christians love the book He authored—*all* of the book He authored! That fact is no little thing. What sort of condescending arrogance is it to study whatever part of it we choose while rejecting the other part or to criticize God for being obtuse and refusing to take the time and pains necessary to understand the divine mind? Is prophecy difficult? Yes and no. Students of prophecy discern that, typically, God gives us enough information to produce hope but not enough to produce arrogance.

    In addition, difficult parts of the Bible have no chance of becoming clear without study. Most people can recall being afraid of attempting to learn a new skill, and then, after a while, coming to be at ease with the task. It is true, of course, that we must wait for the fulfillment of a predicted event to understand the prophecy in its fullest sense. In profound understatement, one writer has said about understanding prophecy: "Difficulties do not set aside revelations; the event will clear up seeming difficulties."[1] We must not, however, refuse to study, say, the doctrine of Heaven simply because it is, in some of its implications, unimaginably profound.

7. When God sends forth a prophecy and then causes it to be fulfilled, it is ultimately a powerful witness to His own glory and majesty. *That may well be, in fact, its essential usefulness.* Consider Isaiah 41:21–29, where the one true God's ability to predict events and bring them to pass is contrasted with the weakness of all other gods who can do neither. God asks, "Who has declared from the beginning that we may know? And former times, that we may say, 'He is righteous?'" (verse 26). God challenges mankind, through Isaiah, to name another god who predicted events and then made them come to pass. The obvious answer is that only the one, true, and living God can do that.

    Later in Isaiah 43:9, God says, "Who among [the nations] can declare this, and show us former things? Let them bring out their witnesses, that they may be justified; or let them hear and say, 'It is truth.'" And still later in Isaiah 48:5, God says, "Even from the beginning I have declared it to you; before it came to pass I proclaimed it to you, lest you should say, 'My idol has done them.'" God seeks His own glory by forcing honest men to confess that He and He alone rules over the affairs of men and nations and that His omniscience allows Him to speak the end from the beginning.

One of the recent theological rages (referred to as "open theism") posits a God who does not precisely know the future and who must wait until events have happened and then attempt to deal redemptively with what He discovers in the process. Such a notion is antithetical to all orthodox teaching about God and has, justifiably, been rejected by biblically-informed Christians.

While prophecy does, indeed, for a variety of reasons, challenge the student, the ancient church knew and knew well the basic outline of things to come. Of course, differences of opinion occurred about some aspects of prophecy, but again, initially, the Church was largely in essential agreement as to what God had promised for the future. Long before it happened, for instance, preachers taught that God had promised to bring the scattered nation of Israel together from the nations of the world, causing persons instructed in prophetic matters to be happy but not surprised on May 14, 1948, when Israel once again became a nation.

Perhaps it would be of utmost prudence for those that write on prophetic themes to leave off the novelties which so clutter the current eschatological scene and to return to the pristine teaching of the early church, which, as we shall see, centered around the return of Christ *following* a period of unprecedented tribulation, at which time He would judge the nations, deliver His people, and establish His millennial kingdom on earth.

PART ONE

**Foundations
of Theory**

How Is It All Going To End?

The universe is finite. It had a beginning, and it will have an ending. That is true, we know, of all energy systems. The "second law of thermodynamics" or "entropy" demands it. It is inevitable. And, since that law functions at all times and in all places, the death-process of our planet is occurring even at this moment.

The Bible does not deny the existence of physical laws such as the second law of thermodynamics. In fact, when we say the phrase, "the second law of thermodynamics," we are only labeling an observable and provable phenomenon which God Himself set in motion at creation.

The Bible, however, does explicitly teach as well as demonstrate that God is able to over-ride His own laws and, at times, does so. Every prayer (except that of praise) is essentially our request for God to override His natural laws and to perform what we call a "miracle." No one ever prays, "Dear Lord, please make the laws that govern human health operate today as usual," because he knows that such a process will occur whether he prays in such a manner or not. He might well, however, pray something like this: "Dear Lord, please heal Johnny," meaning, "Overcome the disease process and the usual healing process by whatever means are at your disposal," which means, obviously, that he is praying for a miracle, a suspension of natural law or at least of "natural" law as he understands it.

Now, how does this relate to the failure of our solar system? Again, all knowledgeable people concur that if things continue as they are, the death of the solar system is inevitable. However, all Bible students know that God has something else planned for the future of our world, something that overrides the natural processes which would otherwise end our existence. These students know that God will end human history on this planet by sending His Son Jesus back to the earth before the otherwise inevitable death of the natural order sets in. Jesus' return and the events surrounding it will be the concluding chapter of history as we know it.

Prevalence and Pattern

How often does the Bible speak of these "end times" or, as the theologians call them, these "eschatological" (from the Greek *eschatos,* meaning the last or final) events? To repeat, leading students of prophecy are generally agreed that between 25% and 30% of the Bible is comprised of predictive prophecy.

Pattern

We have said that the end of our world as we now know it will come when Jesus returns to earth. It is more helpful, however, to put it this way: our world will end with a set of events, a cluster of events, the central focus of which is Jesus Christ's return to earth.

The following represents the essential order of end-time events prophesied in the Bible as understood by Bible students throughout the ages:

1. By means of the preaching of the Gospel of Christ to people around the globe, many millions will come to believe the gospel, but toward the end of human history, a "great falling away" or a "great rebellion," an apostasy from the truth, will occur.

2. At that time, a period of unprecedented trouble (produced by Satan working through a person called "the antichrist") will occur. This period will last seven years, the last half of which is called "the great tribulation." It will affect the Jews (the period being "a time of Jacob's trouble" according to Jeremiah 30:7), but it will also affect the remaining billions of people on the globe who are not Jews. The difficulties of the period

will grow in intensity, and toward the end, God will execute His wrath on the earth.

3. At least by the midpoint of the seven-year period, Satan's agent, the antichrist, will be known and recognized. It is predicted that he will cause "the abomination of desolation" (or the "abomination which desolates"), which refers to his offering an unacceptable sacrifice in defiance of the Jews in the reconstructed temple in Jerusalem. In those last three-and-a-half years, millions will be slain, but millions will also be saved. Many but not all Christians will die. Thus, three events are to occur before Christ's return: the apostasy or falling away from the truth, the tribulation, and the manifestation of antichrist. (Some who hold such general views, however, do not believe in a rebuilt temple in Jerusalem.)

4. At the end of the tribulation, cosmological signs will occur, and then "the sign of the Son of Man in heaven" will happen. That is, Jesus will literally return to the earth. Otherwise stated, end-time orthodoxy for the early church fathers was post-tribulational and pre-millennial. That is, *the Church believed it would go through the tribulation period after which Christ would return to establish His millennial reign.*

5. As Jesus descends to the earth at the end of the tribulation, it was believed, the saved dead will rise from their graves and the living saved will be "raptured," i.e., taken up alive from the earth to meet Christ. *This is the first resurrection.* The ones resurrected (the saved dead) and the ones raptured (the saved living) will then descend to earth with Christ to defeat antichrist and destroy the nations that he, the antichrist, had previously led in battle against God's people. This event is called the battle of Armageddon because of its presumed location at Megiddo. In that crisis, at Christ's return, millions of unbelieving Jews will immediately accept Christ as their Messiah as they "look upon Him whom they have pierced," according to Zechariah 12:10. Many millions of Gentiles will also be saved.

6. It was commonly held that then Jesus will destroy the nations and set up His rule for a thousand years on earth with Jerusalem as His capital. This is "the millennium." The duration of this time of peace and prosperity is specifically mentioned only in Revelation 20:2–7 where we are told on six occasions of the thousand-year period, the "millennium" (a compound of two Latin words, *mille* and *annus*), literally meaning a thousand years. (Although the word is used only in Revelation twenty, many of the prophets spoke of a golden age of peace, prosperity, and security which will come after Israel's severe judgments at the end of the age.)

7. At the end of the millennium, a revolt ("Gog and Magog") involving rebels from all over the earth will occur and will be put down suddenly by Jesus (Revelation 20:7–10).

8. At that time, which will be at the end of the millennial period following the "Gog and Magog" revolt, the remainder of the dead (the unsaved dead) will be resurrected. This is the second resurrection. The unsaved dead will have been in their graves during Christ's thousand-year reign. Then the final judgment, the "great white throne" judgment, will occur, and eternity will be ushered in with all who have ever lived being sent forever either to Heaven or to Hell.

Such was, in basic outline, the theology of last things which the early church commonly taught. It can properly be labeled "orthodoxy," a true expression of the faith once delivered to the saints. It is historically accurate to say that the foregoing represents apostolic teaching—a pre-millennial return of Christ following a period of tribulation.

New Doctrines

What are the basic teachings regarding Christ's Second Coming being espoused today? Do they all agree with the outlines just presented? Do all predict a literal tribulation period, a literal return of Christ after such a time, a literal reign of Christ on earth for a thousand years, and so forth? The answer is in the negative. Some of the most popular end-time theologies being taught today are as follows:

1. *Post-millennialism* teaches that Jesus will actually come to earth again but that the power of the gospel will so permeate the culture that the day will come when most of the people on earth will be saved or at least acknowledge Jesus' authority. At some point thereafter, Jesus will come and personally take over the management of the universe. Thus, post-millennialism contends that Jesus will come after the millennium and not before it.

   The origin of this teaching is often attributed to Daniel Whitby (1638–1726), an Anglican minister and prolific writer. He taught that the world would be converted, the Jews would return to their homeland, and all enemies of the gospel, including the "Papacy" and the Muslims, would be defeated, and then Christ would come. The doctrine became the dominant teaching in the Church for about two hundred years until just after the turn of the twentieth century.

   The belief has waned due to the two global wars (and scores of other limited and regional conflicts) as well as widespread moral decline, even decadence, and few would defend it today. It must be remembered that post-millennialists are post-tribulational and, therefore, teach that Jesus will come at the end of any troubles which, in any sense, pertain to the Bible's predicted end-time tribulation period.

2. *A-millennialism* teaches an actual and literal return of Christ but that there will not be an actual earthly millennium, a period of peace and prosperity as many Old Testament prophecies predict. Thus, this view is labeled a-millennial or *non*-millennial, the alpha (the English letter *a*) negating a word in the Greek language, as in "theist" and "atheist." A-millennialists admit the prophecies of a golden age but spiritualize them (or allegorize them or idealize them) and define the millennium, such as it is, as occurring now during the Church Age. Some say it is not happening on earth but in Heaven. Other variations in the teaching occur, but the essence contends that there is no actual reign of Christ on earth for a thousand years.

This view remains popular in some circles. It originated with Augustine in the fourth century when he allegorized passages dealing with a supposed future reign of Christ on earth. It was, in fact, the dominant view for about a thousand years. Again, it is important to remember that, though such is not the faith of the primitive church, a-millennialists are post-tribulational, so they believe Christ will come after any "tribulational" (however defined) troubles.

3. *Pre-millennialism* holds that Christ will literally appear on earth again one day and that His return will signal the beginning of His thousand year reign on earth with, many believe, Jerusalem as His capital. Thus, "pre-millennialism" teaches that He will return before His millennial reign. This view can be traced to the earliest church fathers, dating back to the time of the apostles themselves. Historically speaking, no other eschatology (with a literal biblical base) was propounded until Augustine's a-millennialism in the fourth century. Many, however, insist that Augustine's allegorizing disallows his view from being labeled as truly biblical.

During the first three centuries of the Christian era, pre-millennialism appears to have been the dominant eschatological interpretation. Among its adherents were Papias, Irenaeus, Justin Martyr, Tertullian, Hippolytus, Methodius, Commodianus and Lactantius.[2] Therefore, to truly defend the eschatology of the early church fathers is to defend pre-millennialism. The church fathers, parenthetically, are usually thought of as approximately two hundred men who wrote from the end of the apostolic age until about 300 AD.

Because the view was taught by the earliest Christian writers, it is called "historic pre-millennialism" and was not only the dominant view of the Church throughout the early centuries, but even those who espouse other views such a "pre-tribulational" pre-millennialism admit that today it continues to be in the ascendancy.

Before moving on to the specific focus of this book, let us ask: what are the essential arguments for a pre-millennial interpretation of end-time events as opposed to post-millennialism and a-millennialism?

First, a pre-millennial view was the explicit faith of the early church. "No man before Augustine offers a creative interpretation of Revelation 20 other than the natural one (i.e., a literal thousand year reign). Furthermore, Justin Martyr tells us that chiliastic (millennial) doctrine was practically normative and an essential element of orthodox doctrine."[3] Second, pre-millennialism takes the Scriptures, both in the Old Testament and in the New Testament, relating to end-time events in their most literal and common-sense meaning. Third, it offers the most, perhaps even only, coherent and harmonious correlation of all biblical passages dealing with eschatology.

A new pre-millennialism, to be distinguished from "historic pre-millennialism" just described, arose in the first quarter of the nineteenth century. It was first mentioned in writing in about 1830. It added certain unfamiliar aspects to historic pre-millennialism, the most significant being that, though Christ will come before the millennium, He will have taken His

Church away from the earth seven years before the inauguration of His millennial reign, and thus, a "pre-tribulation rapture" will occur.

A television preacher, while exegeting a passage in the Book of Revelation, recently said, "Of course, at this point, the Church will have already been raptured." We shall now turn to the question, "Upon what basis does his 'of course' stand?"

A *Second* Second Coming

T he author is quite at pains, early on, to establish in the mind of the reader what was until about 170 years ago the essential rudiments of orthodox, biblically-based eschatology—"post-tribulational pre-millennialism." The Second Advent of Christ is to occur at the end of the tribulation and serves not only to raise the dead saints and rapture the living ones, not only to defeat antichrist and his forces, but also to signal the inauguration of Christ's thousand-year reign of peace on earth. Such was the teaching of the early church fathers and was based, they said, on the clear teaching of Scripture.

Now, let us compare the foregoing view, which is understood to be the orthodox view for the first two or three centuries after Jesus' ascension and presently to be the most popular one, with the following outline which appeared recently in a well-known national religious journal. This outline represents the "pre-tribulation" view of Christ's Second Coming and the (precise) sequence in which these end-time events will occur according to those who hold the view:

1. The rapture of the Church (1 Thessalonians 4:13–18)

2. The revival of the Roman Empire (Daniel 7:7, 24)

3. The rise of the antichrist (Revelation 13:1–18)

4. The apostate world church (Revelation 17:1–15)

5. A seven-year peace treaty with Israel (Daniel 9:25–27)

6. The peace treaty with Israel broken (Daniel 7:23, 9:25–27)

7. Martyrdom of those who refuse to worship the beast (Revelation 13:1–15)

8. Divine judgments: seals, trumpets, and bowls (Revelation 6–18)

9. A world war culminating in the battle of Armageddon (Revelation 18:12–16)

10. The triumphal return of Christ (Revelation 19:11–21)

11. The millennial kingdom (Revelation 10:1–6)

12. The great white throne judgment (Revelation 20:11–15)

13. Eternity: new heaven and a new earth (Revelation 21:1–2)[4]

Note that, though expressed a bit differently and with the addition of various details, the essential difference with this outline and what the Church has historically taught and believed appears at the top of the list: "The rapture of the Church (1 Thessalonians 4:13–18)." Another addition would be the suggestion by item number seven on the list that all who do not worship the Antichrist will be martyred; many will but not all as we shall see.

That event, we are told repeatedly by those who accept the doctrine of a pre-tribulational rapture of the Church is "the next event on God's timetable." It triggers all the events which follow, so they cannot occur until such a rapture happens. All other eschatological events wait upon it. Every Christian is supposed to be watching not for the "final" coming of Christ but for a coming (or an "approaching") seven years earlier. The Church, in this view, will not be on earth during the tribulation period. This new doctrine was superimposed by an unusual set of events on the doctrine of last things held by the early church:

> The program of prophetic events which (pre-tribulationists) taught (when they devised the doctrine in the early 19th century) included important elements which are not found in the early church. Among these were the teachings of the Rapture of the Church at the beginning of the Tribulation and the expectation of

an any-moment secret coming of Christ for the purpose of the rap-
turing of the Church.[5]

At the outset of any discussion of these matters, it is important to understand two facts: (a) When the early church leaders taught that Jesus would
appear after the tribulation and before the millennium, they saw no disparity or incongruity between the two doctrines, no reason why events could
not happen in that order. That was, to them, the clear teaching of Scripture.
(b) When pre-tribulationists say that Christ's coming is "imminent," they
mean that no prophesied event stands in the way of His coming. And, they
believe, it has been that way since Jesus ascended to Heaven. He could have
returned immediately after His ascension, He could have returned at any
moment since then, and He can return at any moment now.

That is imminence, according to the pre-tribulationists—an imminence
which most pre-tribulationists state explicitly is at the very heart of their
teaching. Without imminence, so defined, one simply cannot have pre-
tribulational pre-millennialism. However, as we shall see, neither the New
Testament or the writings of the early church mentions any such doctrine.

Perhaps it will be helpful to state here that pre-tribulationists almost always
designate themselves with the word *dispensational*. The teaching that God
deals at different times ("dispensations") in different ways with different
peoples need not concern us at the moment, although, as we shall see, it is
a crucial facet of pre-tribulationism.

It is critically important, however, to distinguish between pre-millennialism
and dispensational pre-tribulational pre-millennialism; the two are not synonymous but are substantively different. That must be kept in mind because
pre-tribulationalists commonly attempt to equate pre-tribulationalism with
pre-millennialism. However, the historical fact is that pre-millennialism
was taught over 1800 years before anybody ever knew of a pre-tribulational
rapture pre-millennialism.

So, where then did the teaching of a pre-tribulational rapture come from?
When was it added to what had been the essential eschatology of the

Church? Does the Bible teach such an event? The author quoted who placed the pre-tribulational rapture at the top of his list of things to come says that 1 Thessalonians 4:13–18 teaches such an event. Is that true? Does that passage or any other in the entirety of the Bible teach such? It is to that question that we now turn.

The History of the Pre-tribulational Rapture Doctrine

The specific purpose of the first portion of this book is to examine the various passages commonly held to teach pre-tribulationism. Before we deal with such passages, however, some basic historical facts about the origin and development of the doctrine of pre-tribulationism might be helpful.

First, there is no evidence whatsoever that anybody before the early 1830s had ever known such a doctrine. That, in itself, does not make the doctrine true or false, but it is of great importance to realize that the first perpetrators of the doctrine themselves called it "new" and not a recovery of earlier truth. A silence about such an event for the first 1800 years of church history is a momentous fact. It is the "dog that didn't bark."

It is almost impossible to conceive that God would have hidden such a pivotal event, which some label one of the "fundamentals of the Christian faith," from all believers for most of Christian history. Though many thousands of pages were written on various doctrines of the faith during the first several hundred years after the apostles died, including much on eschatology, no evidence exists to suggest that anybody ever thought of a pre-tribulational return of Christ until after the first quarter of the 19th century.

Second, there is much well-documented evidence that the doctrine was first taught publicly in September 1830 in Edward Irving's journal *The*

Morning Watch in London, England, by a writer identified only as "Fidus." It was also a doctrine in the "Catholic Apostolic Church" which Irving founded. Irving himself first taught such an event in June 1831 in the same journal, and he was almost surely influenced in coming to believe the doctrine by a Scottish girl named Margaret Macdonald who had experienced a vision of a split-second coming, first for those who were spiritually prepared (before the coming of the "evil one") and later for those church members who were not sufficiently spiritually prepared and who, therefore, would be forced to experience the tribulation period.

John Nelson Darby, whose writings had no clear pre-tribulational teaching before 1839, helped found a church called the "Brethren" in the United Kingdom. In the early days of the life of that fellowship, it gave nurture and impetus to the theory. Darby popularized the teaching both in the United Kingdom and (beginning in about 1862) in America, and he saw it grow ever more familiar by means of the "Bible School" movement and, most powerfully, by the Scofield Bible.

Cyrus Ingerson Scofield (1843–1921) learned the doctrine of the pre-tribulational return of Christ from the Brethren and also heavily bought in to "dispensationalism." His book *Rightly Dividing the Word of Truth* among other things, delineates and defines the seven dispensations of the dispensational interpretation of the Bible. No one, he says, can hope to properly interpret the Scriptures without knowing to which of his seven dispensations to assign a biblical passage.[6] The booklet was widely read, but it was the Bible he edited that was the most effective instrument, particularly in America, for the spreading of both dispensationalism and pre-tribulationism.

Published first in 1909, a second edition appeared in 1917, and a committee of nine edited yet a third edition which appeared in 1967. Famous for its notes, it sold many millions of copies and continues to be a favorite, indeed, the only acceptable Bible to many.

An indication of the influence of Scofield and his Bible notations is the fact that even *today* while listening to a taped Bible message, I heard a speaker, a well-known pastor of one of the largest churches in America, say in dead earnest, "To save a bit of time finding the passage for the text of my message, turn to page 336 in the old Scofield Bible," meaning the 1909 version.

People interested in the general matter are well-advised to check out modern writers on the subject of the origin of the teaching. In several books, Dave MacPherson delineates the history of the doctrine. MacPherson, a reporter for newspapers, radio, and television for over two decades, is noted for his meticulous research into his favorite subject—biblical eschatology. He is a prolific writer, and in several books, including *The Incredible Cover-up* and *The Rapture Plot,* he chronicles the origins and early days of the doctrine. The desperate attempts of pre-tribulationists, both in the past and in the present, to cover up the truth about the origin of the teaching in order to attribute it to Darby and not to Margaret Macdonald or Edward Irving is the focus of his book *The Rapture Plot.* Pre-tribulationists find it difficult to admit that Miss Macdonald had any part in the doctrine's origin because she experienced charismatic gifts (though after she saw her pre-tribulational partial rapture), and they do not want to admit that Irving had anything to do with it because he was later defrocked by his denomination for holding heretical views on the person of Christ.

Concerning the doctrine's origin, MacPherson concludes based upon his intricate study that "the Irvingites publicly taught a pre-tribulational rapture long before Darby did." He also holds that until the late 1830's (after Miss Macdonald had received her visions and after the *Morning Watch* had begun voicing the new pre-tribulational view) Darby only anticipated the Revelation chapter nineteen coming.

MacPherson quotes Robert Cameron:

> On the authority of the late Dr. S. P. Tregelles [a brilliant Bible scholar among the Brethren], whom the learned Rendel Harris has called 'the greatest Biblical Scholar of the Nineteenth Century,' no mention is found in any Christian literature extant, from the first century until AD 1830, making mention of these modern (pre-

tribulational) teachings. All the 'great Teachers,' all 'the most spiritually minded,' and the whole body of Christians prior to the days of Edward Irving, were a unit in believing that the Church would not escape the Tribulation.[7]

Again, according to *The Encyclopedia of Christianity*, the originator of this tradition of biblical interpretation is John Nelson Darby (1800–1882), an Anglican priest who was the leader of a group of separatist believers who later became known as the Plymouth Brethren. Darby was a "futurist" in his eschatology, believing that the biblical prophecies of the last days were yet to be fulfilled. In the 1830s and 1840s, he developed two distinctive additions to futurist thinking: (1) the Church Age was a "parenthesis" between the 69th and 70th "weeks" of years in Daniel 9:25–27, and (2) there would be a rapture (so-called from the Vulgate term for "caught up" in 1 Thessalonians 4:17) of believers from the earth to Heaven by Christ before the seventieth week of Daniel nine, the "great tribulation" of divine wrath poured out on human wickedness and unbelief. These two affirmations seem to be genuine novelties in the history of theology, though some have claimed to find seminal elements of them in early thinkers.[8]

From time to time, it is alleged that others believed the doctrine in earlier times, but an honest assessment of the "proof" thoroughly disproves the claim. The four most substantive offerings pre-tribulationists cite of those who supposedly earlier taught the doctrine are some of the church fathers as well as an eighteenth-century Jesuit priest named Manuel Lacunza (1731–1801), pseudo-Ephraem, who wrote between the fourth and seventh centuries, and a certain Morgan Edwards, a British pastor who emigrated to America and who published a book on prophecy in 1788.

First, it is highly informative, even if the aforementioned did indeed teach a pre-tribulational rapture, that there were so few proponents of the doctrine. In fact, as the material in the books listed in the bibliography patently demonstrate, neither the church fathers nor Lacunza nor pseudo-Ephraem (nor the true Ephraem, the Syrian who wrote in the fourth century and from whom the pseudo-Ephraem obtained his basic theology) nor Morgan Edwards—nor anyone else—ever taught the doctrine. MacPherson has done a substantive service to the Church by the reporting his findings about this matter; he conclusively proves from their own writings that none of these men claimed as pre-tribulationists believed or taught the doctrine and that attempts to demonstrate that they did are serious distortions of their provable doctrinal positions.

One of the saddest aspects of the subject is the way in which the teachings of the church fathers and others of the faith have been distorted in an attempt to claim them for pre-tribulationism. The use of the term *distortion* is meant to describe the actual changing of words as well as in some cases deleting key sentences in which the fathers explicitly taught that the Church will be on earth during the tribulation. One notices that recent defenders of pre-tribulationism rarely if ever quote the fathers because having done so has proven such an embarrassment to their forebears. It is a serious charge, but it is obviously true as even a cursory perusal of the relevant materials will demonstrate.

For a candid report of that lamentable process, now thankfully largely over, Gundry in *The Church and the Tribulation* quotes from chapter sixteen of "The Teaching of the Twelve Apostles" (or "Didache," a Greek word for "teaching"), which is a document dating to the last half of the first century: "Watch for your life's sake. Let not your lamps be quenched, nor your loins unloosed; but be ye ready, for ye know not the hour in which our Lord cometh."[9] At this point, many pre-tribulationists, including John F. Walvoord, Gerald B. Stanton, and J. Dwight Pentecost, end their quotations in an endeavor to make the passage establish a belief in imminence—according to their definition—by the early church. However, the document continues to state: "For the whole time of your faith will not profit you, if ye be not made perfect in the last time...then shall appear the world-deceiver as Son of God, and shall do signs and wonders...Then shall the creation of men come into the fire, and many shall be made to stumble and perish; but they that endure in their faith shall be saved from under the curse itself."[10]

Unfortunately, several pre-tribulationists, in an attempt to bolster their position, have not hesitated to distort what the church fathers and others taught. In fact, it is a common facet of their writings. Again, I refer to MacPherson's *The Rapture Plot* with its fascinating account of how pre-tribulationists, early and modern, have knowingly distorted history, even going so far as to change words of Christian hymns in order to re-write history. The entirety of his *The Three R's: Rapture, Revisionism, and Robbery* is a riveting, if sad, account of the plagiarism employed by some of the most verbal proponents of the movement. Several other authors offer lists of the church fathers who explicitly taught a post-tribulational return of Christ.[11]

Interestingly, H. C. Thiessen, well-known pre-tribulational theologian, says that the fathers taught imminence, but he then admits that they did so only because they thought they might already be in the tribulation period. He then says there are "hints" that they taught that the Church might miss the tribulation but that they elsewhere explicitly taught that the Church will go through the tribulation. However, the "hints," upon careful perusal, prove to be evanescent.[12]

The Fathers were, in fact, uniformly pre-millennial and post-tribulational, and many of them taught it explicitly, though, again, some clear-cut statements are often deliberately deleted or suffer word changes by pre-tribulationists who quote them. It is true that the fathers often spoke of a sense of Christ's imminent return but that was because they thought they might be living in the tribulation period already. Again, as we have seen, these church fathers, parenthetically, are usually thought of as approximately 200 men who wrote from the end of the apostolic age until about 300 AD. The immediate successors of the apostles, the post-apostolic fathers, wrote in the first and second centuries, and apologists wrote in the second century, and polemicists (those who argued against heresies) wrote in the late second and third centuries. It is essential, however, to note that these fathers did not hold to an "imminence" which said that Jesus would come before certain clear-cut signs occurred.

Following is a representative quote which could be multiplied almost end-lessly, concerning the eschatology of the early church fathers:

> The antiquity of a view [post-tribulationism] weighs in its favor, especially when that antiquity reaches back to the apostolic age. For those who received their doctrine first-hand from the apostles and from those who heard them stood in a better position to judge what was apostolic doctrine than we who are many centuries removed. Until Augustine in the fourth century, the early church generally held to the premillenarian understanding of Biblical eschatology. This chiliasm (*mille* is Latin for a thousand, and *kilias* is Greek for a thousand) entailed a futuristic interpretation of Daniel's seventieth week, the abomination of desolation, and the personal Antichrist. And it was posttribulational. Neither men-tioned or considered, the possibility of a pretribulational rapture seems never to have occurred to anyone in the early church.[13]

In an interesting attempt to lump all of the church fathers into the same camp, John Walvoord writes: "In a word, the early Fathers were not specif-ically pre-tribulational, neither were they all post-tribulational in the mod-ern meaning of the term...It may, therefore, be concluded that while the early church did not teach twentieth-century pre-tribulationism neither did it clearly teach modern post-tribulationism.[14] As we have seen, the only church fathers who were not demonstrably post-tribulational were the few who did not address the issue. Furthermore, while we may debate the use of the terms *clearly* and *modern,* the fact is, as we have shown, the church fathers' post-tribulationism differs in no substantive way from what mod-ern post-tribulationists teach.

In addition, later in the sixteenth and seventeenth centuries, the reformers taught what is known as the "protestant view" which held that the 1260 days of tribulation should be understood as years (the "year-day" theory) and that the entire sweep of church history should be seen as the time frame of the promised tribulation. Thus, it was *historicist;* that is, it was to occur throughout the entirety of church history and was not seen as being futuristic. That, of course, was contrary to what orthodox eschatology had always held.

The theory of the 1260 days of the tribulational period representing 1260 years is commonly attributed to a Roman Catholic priest named Joachim of Fiore who lived in the 1100s. When, however, more than 1260 years passed (no matter when the various schools began the countdown), the teaching fell into disfavor. One of the salutary results of that disfavor was a renewed interest in futurism, the view held uniformly by the early church, and it was into this renewed interest in futurism that Miss Macdonald, Edward Irving (and his Catholic Apostolic Church), and J. N. Darby (and the "Brethren" or "Plymouth Brethren" as they are sometimes called) came into prominence with their "imminency" and "pre-tribulationalism."

Both those who accepted pre-tribulationism and those who rejected it— and there were many among the Brethren, notably the very able S. P. Tregelles and B. W. Newton who did so from the beginning—said it was something altogether new and not a rediscovery of earlier doctrine. To say, as it often is, that pre-tribulationism is but a recovery of ancient doctrine is essentially to deconstruct history. The ancient doctrine of pre-millennialism was, indeed, recovered, but a new theory called pre-tribulationism was then added to it.

PART TWO

The Biblical Materials

Biblical Foundations
for Belief

A gain, our specific interest is to ask, "What are the most favored verses used in an attempt to establish the legitimacy of the doctrine of the pre-tribulation rapture?" One hears certain "proof" texts constantly quoted; they are touted as proof-positive evidence that Jesus will rapture His Church away from the earth seven years before the actual Second Coming. Instead of taking the passages in the order in which they appear in the New Testament, we will take them in the order in which one customarily hears them quoted by current pre-tribulationists. We shall observe, in fact, that not one of them says anything about a pre-tribulational rapture and, indeed, that some of them explicitly teach post-tribulationalism. We shall note further the obvious way in which many of them have been distorted in an attempt to deny their obvious meaning.

1 Thessalonians 4:13–18

"But I do not want you to be ignorant, brethren, concerning those who have fallen asleep, lest you sorrow as others who have no hope. For if we believe that Jesus died and rose again, even so God will bring with Him those who sleep in Jesus. But this we say to you by the word of the Lord, that we who are alive and remain until the coming of the Lord will by no means precede those who are asleep. For the Lord Himself will descend from heaven with a shout, with the voice of an archangel, and with the trumpet of God. And the dead in Christ will rise first. Then we who are alive and remain shall be caught up together with them in the clouds to meet the Lord in the air. And thus we shall always be with the Lord. Therefore comfort one another with these words."

This passage is surely the one most commonly used to prove a pre-tribulation rapture. John Walvoord, in his well-known defense of pre-tribulationism titled *The Rapture Question,* offers two texts, 1 Corinthians 15:51–52 and 1 Thessalonians 4:13–18 as his foundational texts proving, he avers, the pre-tribulational rapture.

In commenting on another favorite verse of pre-tribulationists (Revelation 4:1f), which states, "And I will show you things which must take place after this...," Warren Wiersbe says: "It would appear that...John illustrates what will happen to God's people when the Church Age has run its course: heaven will open; there will be a voice and the sound of a trumpet; and the saints will be caught up to heaven."[1]

Warren Wiersbe, former pastor of Moody Church in Chicago, is a well-known writer and speaker and is one of the best-known modern evangelicals. He has written over eighty books and is known for his preaching ministry through the "Back to the Bible" radio broadcast. Wiersbe attempts to prove the pre-tribulational rapture by citing two texts: 1 Corinthians 15:52 and 1 Thessalonians 4:13–18. Accordingly, the majority if not all pre-tribulationists use these two passages as being the two most substantive in the New Testament in teaching a pre-tribulational rapture. In fact, many pre-tribulationists say that 1 Thessalonians 4:13–18 is the primary verse upon which their theory is established because it is here, they say, that a pre-tribulational rapture was revealed for the first time in history to Paul.

In fact, neither passage has anything to say about a pre-tribulational rapture. Both passages favor the historic post-tribulational position and fit it perfectly with the latter, *requiring* such unless the meaning of the passage is radically changed from the context in which it was given. Let the question then be asked: "Can this passage be properly used to demonstrate a pre-tribulational rapture?"

The central message of the text (in regard to Christ's coming) is this: we are told that all the saved (both raised and raptured) will meet the Lord in the air, but we are not told what happens next.

Any one of many events might occur next. Believers might continue in an upward direction into the skies with Christ (as pre-tribulationists say), or they might descend with Christ to the earth for the battle of Armageddon (as the Church has historically taught), but in any case, we are simply not told what happens after meeting Christ, and therefore, the passage should never be used to "prove" either a post-tribulational return of Christ or a pre-tribulational return of Christ. Paul simply does not tell us what happens next. It may be that he does elsewhere in the New Testament, but that remains to be seen.

To put it another way, the question could legitimately be asked, "At what specific point in the passage—after which word or clause—is the subject of a pre-tribulational return of Christ mentioned?" No such information is given in the text which is surely why Walvoord nowhere in his *The Rapture Question* actually exegetes the passage, a remarkable fact in view of its pivotal importance, in his view, to the establishment of the doctrine. [2]

We are customarily told that the pre-tribulational rapture was not taught in the Old Testament but was revealed to Paul as a "mystery" and that it was in this place in which Paul first revealed the rapture to the Church. Two facts about such a statement must be kept in mind: (a) a "mystery" in the New Testament is something that has been hidden but is now revealed; it is an *open secret*. The mystery of the Church, which God vouchsafed Paul, is not about a pre-tribulational rapture but about God creating a new body of people in which Jews and Gentiles can become unified by the power of God—thus creating the Church itself. (b) The true mystery of a pre-tribulational rapture is that it is never explicitly stated anywhere in the Bible, either in the Old or New Testament. Therefore, if God revealed such a teaching to Paul, it remained his personal secret.

According to pre-tribulationists, there are actually three comings of Christ: the first has already occurred, and the second one is the "secret and signless rapture" of the saints in which Jesus comes but doesn't; that is, He comes all the way from Heaven to earth but doesn't quite touch the earth. Instead, He takes His Church back to Heaven with Him (or remains in the skies with the Church). The third is His coming at the end of the tribulation, at the very end of history. (The early contention of a "secret and signless" rapture among pre-tribulationists has been modified by some modern pre-tribulationists as we will see.)

The problem is that the New Testament calls His coming in the air "the coming of the Lord" (1 Thessalonians 4:15). Upon what basis shall we change the meaning of the word in that verse and redefine it as a "coming" which is not a "coming"? Actually, in the view of the theorists, one is an "approaching" and the other is an actual "coming."

The Greek word used for "coming" here is *parousia,* a word that is commonly used, pre-tribulationists admit, for Christ's final coming as well as what they term the pre-tribulational rapture which, in their view, occurs seven years earlier. In fact, early pre-tribulationists, because of their new doctrine, were forced to speak of a third coming as well as a second coming. Some even spoke of a "first-first resurrection" and a "second-first resurrection."

Another very interesting facet of this text (and one that favors post-tribulationism) involves the word in 1 Thessalonians 4:17 translated "meet." Various authors have cited the provable fact that this Greek word, *apantesis,* is used only three other times in the entire New Testament, and in all three passages, it refers to a "meeting and returning with." It is used in Matthew 25:6 when the virgins go out to meet the bridegroom and immediately return with him to the wedding. It is used in Acts 28:15–16, which records Christians going out to meet Paul on his way to Rome, turning, and accompanying him back to the city, and it is used here to picture Christ's descent with believers being raptured to meet Him in the air, turning, and then accompanying Him to earth. The word *parousia,* in its first-century setting, was used to refer to a visit by a dignitary of some sort and the process of the citizenry going out to meet him. When the people met him and turned again to re-enter the city, that act was called the *apantesis,* that is "to meet and return with." That accords with the ancient teaching of the Church that believers will meet Christ in His *parousia* and turn and immediately return with Him back to the earth in an *apantesis.*

In Walvoord's classic pre-tribulational volume, *The Rapture Question,* he does not exegete the meaning of *apantesis,* and in Pentecost's voluminous *Things to Come,* the author simply denies the lexical meaning of the word but does not quote any lexicon.

The historic faith is that there is one Second Coming in which Jesus resurrects or raptures away all the saved, meets them in the air, and then continues His descent to earth to defeat the nations and to establish His millennial rule. But again, while this passage is in perfect accord with that teaching, it does not explicitly explain what Jesus does following our meeting in the air.

Much light is thrown on the entire matter if one continues reading into chapter five in which the apostle says nothing at all about looking for a pre-tribulational rapture, but rather, he encourages his readers to live in obedience to the faith until the end-time events happen.

Paul continues his message to the Thessalonians and indicates that we "are not in darkness, so that this Day should overtake us as a thief." (5:4) What "day"? The day of Christ, the day of the Lord (5:2), the day of Christ's Second Coming to judge the nations. What a perfect place for the apostle to inform us that we won't be overtaken as a thief in the night precisely because we will already have been secretly raptured away, but he doesn't do that. He could have said as the television preacher said: "Of course, at this point, the Church will have already been raptured." But he says none of that. His encouragement? To watch and be sober (5:6), to put on the "breastplate of faith and love and as a helmet the hope of salvation" (5:8), all of which is meaningless if we won't be here but very pertinent if we will.

The apostle says that the day will come on Christians then living, but it will not overtake them as a thief! If the theorist is right, Christians will not even experience the day, and so what Paul wrote here is not only gratuitous, it is nonsensical. Interestingly, John the apostle uses this same "thief" coming of Christ in Revelation 16:15 which, all are agreed, is the final coming of Christ at the onset of Armageddon. Thus, all is clear and consistent if we hold to the ancient teaching of a single second return of Christ at the end of history.

As to the word *day* as in "the day of Christ," "the day of Christ Jesus," and "the day of the Lord," Walvoord admits (as most modern pre-tribulationists do) that they refer to the same day, except when pre-tribulationists choose to attach them to either the Rapture or the "revelation" which is to occur seven years later at the return in glory.

Sometimes, Walvoord says, we must interpret "the day of the Lord" as referring to the day of Christ coming in judgment seven years after the pre-tribulational rapture and not to the rapture itself. How do we know when to do that? We know to do that when the criteria arbitrarily established for the final "day of the Lord" are met.

But what about 1 Thessalonians 5:9 where Paul says, "For God did not appoint us to wrath, but to obtain salvation through the Lord Jesus Christ?" In this often quoted passage, we are told by pre-tribulationists that the wrath from which God promises to save us is the wrath of antichrist or His own wrath which befalls the earth during the tribulation. God plans to deliver us before the beginning of the tribulation, they say, in fulfillment of the promise stated here. However, that interpretation is based on an assumption and not upon a statement of fact. One must come to the passage with a pre-tribulational bias (what logicians call an "antecedent predisposition") to so interpret it in that manner.

Other possibilities present themselves as to the definition of the "wrath" from which He promises to deliver us. Whose wrath does the apostle speak of? Man's wrath, the devil's wrath, antichrist's wrath, or God's wrath? And does it speak of tribulational wrath on earth or God's eternal wrath in Hell? It must be remembered that God will express His wrath in the tribulation (Revelation 15:1, 16:1, and 19:15), Christ will express His wrath there (Revelation 6:16), Satan will express his wrath there, (Revelation 12:12), and evil men will express their wrath there (Revelation 16.6).

It is possible that the tribulational wrath of the antichrist is spoken of in 1 Thessalonians 5:9, but to say so is an inference, a supposition. It is not explicitly stated. The wrath spoken of in this verse may well be as the early church always taught: the eternal wrath of God to which He has certainly not appointed us.

Historic orthodoxy says that Christians will, indeed, experience the wrath of antichrist but not God's wrath, either temporally or, as expressed in His eternal wrath, in Hell. Further, the wrath here may in fact be God's wrath oppressed on earth with the promise of His deliverance through it but without a promise of deliverance by means of a physical rapture.

It is certainly important to note the evidences that the coming of Christ referenced in this passage is designed to give notice of the event to the entire world. Paul says the coming is attended by three things: "For the Lord Himself will descend from heaven with a shout, with the voice of the archangel, and with the trump of God" (1 Thessalonians 4:16).

All of that, particularly the shout, militates against pre-tribulationism because it is a shout with military connotations, indicating Christ's invasion of the earth, and it does not signal a retreat to Heaven or to some safe place in the skies, as per pre-tribulationism. As to the nature of the shout, William Rowlands cites several translations showing it is, indeed, a battle shout. Martin Luther, in his translation of the New Testament, Rowlands says, used a German word for "war-cry." The Vulgate, he says, has "a shout of command...which a general used." Lange has it that "Christ is thereby described as a victorious captain whose order summons to battle for the destruction of His enemies." Darby himself says, "The shout is a military term." Conybeare and Howson translate it, "With a shout of war." Barnes has it, "A great military rush." Rowlands concludes:

> Christ is thereby (by means of the shout) described as a victorious Captain, whose orders summon to battle for the destruction of His enemies...Is it thought that our Lord will 'shout' for the battle, and instead of fighting it, rush His soldiers off the field leaving evil predominate everywhere? Why a battle shout and no battle? Will Antichrist wear out the saints of the Most High after the Lord Himself has shouted His war-cry? Most assuredly not![3]

Simply, no pre-tribulational information whatever is given in the entire passage, and therefore, it is disqualified as a supposed demonstration of such an event. It is to be carefully noted that it is illogical to state, on the one hand, that God would never allow His children to be on earth during the wrath-filled tribulational period and to say, on the other, that multiplied millions of people will be saved and live through the tribulation. Pre-tribulationists almost universally refuse to call such people "Christians," preferring "tribulational saints," but semantics do not solve the problem. Many millions of faithful and true believers, washed in the blood of Christ (Revelation 7:14), obedient to the Lord Jesus and victorious through His shed blood (Revelation 12:11) will live in and through the tribulation. If all that is so, how is it inconsistent to hold the view of the early church that Christians will be on earth through the antichrist's career?

A common charge against God, if He were to leave His children on earth during the tribulation, is that He is a "child-abuser," but are "tribulation saints" His children or not? Have not the martyrs throughout Christian history been His children? Why would Christ (to use their language) "abuse His bride" or allow anybody else to do so? Indeed, why did God allow His Old Testament people to experience troubles—troubles that sometimes cost them their lives? Even if they are not referred to as His "bride," did He or did He not love them?

It does no good to remonstrate that modern persecution is not nearly as severe as it will be in the tribulation. Ask the millions of Sudanese—to mention but one persecuted people group—who lost their families, their belongings, and their own lives if what they suffered and are suffering may be spoken of as "real."

In 1 Thessalonians 4, Paul deals with all believers, living and dead, at the time of Christ's return, promising that the being dead in Christ constitutes no second-class status for them at Jesus' return. Indeed, they will go to Christ before the living do. Then, in chapter five, he instructs those living in the final days on how to live in the light of Christ's coming, but he does not state or even insinuate that they will be raptured away from the earth before the end-time difficulties.

1 Corinthians 15:51–55

"Behold, I tell you a mystery: We shall not all sleep, but we shall all be changed—in a moment, in the twinkling of an eye, at the last trumpet. For the trumpet will sound, and the dead will be raised incorruptible, and we shall be changed. For this corruptible must put on incorruption, and this mortal must put on immortality. So when this corruptible has put on incorruption, and this mortal has put on immortality, then shall be brought to pass the saying that is written: *'Death is swallowed up in victory. O Death, where is your sting? O Hades, where is your victory?'*"

I know of no pre-tribulationist who does not claim that this passage proves the pre-tribulational rapture. Walvoord states, "One of the two main passages on the doctrine of the Rapture in the New Testament is found in 1 Corinthians 15:51–58...The two passages together [meaning 1 Thessalonians 4:13–18 and 1 Corinthians 15:51–58] give a complete answer to the basic questions concerning the Rapture as an important prophetic event."[4]

The events mentioned here—the resurrection of the dead and the rapture of the saints—happen and then and only then does the tribulation occur, or so we are told. But what does the passage actually state? In truth, the two passages which are reputed to give "a complete answer" give no answer at all about a pre-tribulational rapture.

In fact, Paul says explicitly that all believers will not "sleep," meaning die, but that first the dead will be raised, and those living will be "changed," meaning they will be transformed while living. He also states that such a thing will occur very quickly, "in the twinkling of an eye." We should note, however, that he does not say the event will be secret. Paul then tells us that these things will occur at the "last trumpet," which the early church always took to be the same as the other "last trumpet" of the Revelation. Some scholars contend that "we may well equate the 'great trumpet' at the post-tribulational advent in Matthew 24:31, the last trumpet of 1 Corinthians 15:52, the trumpet of God in 1 Thessalonians 4:16, and perhaps the seventh trumpet in Revelation 11:15–18 as well."[5] Therefore, we may ascertain that all the last trumpets mentioned in these Scriptures are the same.[6]

Furthermore, Paul says that all those who are either resurrected or raised will be given their eternal bodies: "For this corruptible must put on incorruption." He then informs us about the chronology of such an event in the final scheme of things: "...Then shall be brought to pass the saying that is written, *'Death shall be swallowed up in victory.'*"

Though the passage fits perfectly with the old teaching of end-time events, that of pre-millennial post-tribulationism, it fairly bristles with problems for the pre-tribulationists who lean so heavily upon it.

First, how can death be said to have been "swallowed up" when countless millions will be slain in the coming tribulation? Patently, there is massive death and destruction to come following this supposed pre-tribulation rapture.

But worse for the theorists is this problem: if it be asked precisely what Old Testament passage this event fulfills, the answer is Isaiah 25:8, where the prophet states: "He will swallow up death in victory." The editors of the pre-tribulational Scofield Reference Bible give the Isaiah reference in the margin and then state: "Some hold that these [Old Testament believers] will be raised with the Church (1 Thessalonians 4:16–17, 1 Corinthians 15:51–53), prior to the tribulation; others hold that it is more harmonious with the Old Testament Scriptures to include the Old Testament believers with those who rise after the tribulation (Revelation 20:4–6) because both Isaiah and Daniel mention the resurrection of the Old Testament saints as taking place following a time of great trouble (Isaiah 26:16–21; Daniel 12:1–3)."[7]

It does not support the theory to say that some hold that Old Testament saints will be raised before Israel's time of trouble. The Old Testament explicitly states otherwise, and it does so in several places. In fact, it is the only deliverance Israel was ever promised. The Old Testament does not equivocate about that issue. But, if they are raised after the tribulation, as Isaiah 25:8 states, the very promise quoted here by Paul, that fact poses serious problems for the pre-tribulationists who wish to claim this passage for their theory.

As to the timing of the rapture of Christians, Paul is intentional here as he quotes Isaiah to indicate that the coming resurrection or rapture for Israel and everybody else fulfills Isaiah's teaching in 25:8, which follows the tribulation. In light of this, the pre-tribulationist must hold that Isaiah spoke explicitly of a *post*-tribulational resurrection for Old Testament saints and that Paul then uses Isaiah's statement to prove a *pre*-tribulational resurrection for New Testament believers. The passage, then, has to do double-duty and inconsistent double-duty at that. It must teach post-tribulationism for the Old Testament saints and pre-tribulationalism for the New Testament saints.

It is truly difficult to imagine that Paul did not see the explicit inconsistency. Both passages, however, fit the facts perfectly if we hold to the Church's ancient teaching that all of the righteous dead of both dispensations will rise from their graves when Jesus returns to defeat the nations and establish His millennial kingdom, which will occur post-tribulationally, and then all of the saved living will be raptured as well.

Further, corroboratively, Paul states earlier in 1 Corinthians 15:23, "But every man in his own order: Christ the first-fruits; afterward they that are Christ's at his coming." Who is it that are "Christ's"? Some of them? A portion of them? Only the tribulation saints? No, but all Christ has ever saved. And at which coming (*parousia*)? The only coming to which believers are ever told to anticipate.

All of this accords with other Old Testament passages relating to the chronology of the resurrection of the righteous dead and the time of Israel's trouble, notably Daniel 12:1–3, another passage quoted by Paul in the first Corinthians passage just cited, and Hosea 13:14. The entirety of Hosea's thirteenth and fourteenth chapters presents the chronology of the entire prophetic witness of the Old Testament by describing first Israel's tribulational period and then God's deliverance of His people. It appears that in scriptural context the only ultimate deliverance from her enemies that the Old Testament saints knew of was after Israel's troubles, post-tribulationally.

Walvoord's position on the timing of the resurrection of the saved of the Old Testament is worth noting. He says that while many pre-tribulationists hold to a post-tribulational resurrection for saved Israelites, "There is a growing tendency to review the question of whether the Old Testament saints are, after all, raised at the same time as the Church." He says that Daniel 12:1–2 "seems" to put the tribulation first for Israel, yet certain "passages dealing with the resurrection of the Church in the New Testament seem to include only the Church." He is bothered, he says, that the clause "the dead in Christ will rise first" does not mention the resurrection of the Old Testament saints.[8]

How does that fact, however, delimit those raised first to New Testament saints only? He is assuming saved Israelites ought to be mentioned, but that is a gratuitous assumption. Paul was dealing with the resurrection of Christians not the Israelites, or it may well be that Paul was, indeed, referring to Israelites as being "in Christ" as well since their salvation is most certainly in Him and only in Him according to Hebrews 9:15.

Walvoord concludes his section on the subject with this: "The best answer to Reese and Ladd [in their acceptance of the Old Testament chronology of the timing of Israel's tribulation and resurrection] is to concede the point that the resurrection of Old Testament saints is after the Tribulation, and to divorce it completely from the translation and resurrection of the Church."[9] First, Walvoord must concede the point to Reese and Ladd because they hold to the explicit Old Testament teaching. Second, why then "divorce it completely from the translation of the Church"? What is the advantage of the divorce if the events occur at the same time? And what is the evidence of such a divorce? The only possible answer is that dispensationalism cannot allow for the Church and Israel to experience anything together. God would then be "dealing with the Church and Israel at the same time," a thing incomprehensible for dispensationalists as we shall see later. The result is that they cannot admit what is patently clear on the issue, which is that all the saved are raptured or resurrected at precisely the same moment.

All in all, the passage in Corinthians has proven to be an obstacle to pre-tribulationists and cannot be legitimately used in a defense of that doctrine. Unless one is committed preconceptually to a pre-tribulational doctrine and does not see the blatant inconsistencies in such a view and the teaching of the passage, it could never be found in that passage, and the passage could, therefore, never be used in any attempt to prove a pre-tribulational return of Christ.

Nevertheless, even if Paul had not quoted any Old Testament passage, the net result would be precisely the same. The passage does not have a scintilla to say about the resurrection or rapture taking place before the tribulation, for in it, we see no mention at all of any period of tribulation.

Walvoord criticizes Gundry for writing "only four or five pages about this passage" and then he, Walvoord, devotes six-and-a-half to it.[10] However, in those pages, he is silent on the two crucial issues for pre-tribulationism in the passage: (a) where does the passage explicitly mention a pre-tribulational rapture, and (b) why does Paul quote an Old Testament passage teaching precisely the opposite of pre-tribulationists if he, Paul, believed in such a thing?

Walvoord spends much of those six-and-a-half pages on common ground with post-tribulationists yet does not deal at all with issues which would conclusively prove pre-tribulationism if such issues were present in the text.

Once again, if we take the passage in its plain meaning, all becomes clear. However, if we superimpose a pre-tribulational meaning on it, it becomes laden with problems.

Revelation 4:1

"After these things I looked, and behold, a door standing open in heaven. And the first voice which I heard was like a trumpet speaking with me, saying, 'Come up here, and I will show you things which must take place after this.'"

One of pre-tribulationists' favorite passages along with Revelation 3:20 is Revelation 4:1. This verse is so central to the theorists' argument that, in order to determine the eschatological position of any commentary on Revelation, one needs only to look at an author's interpretation of Revelation 4:1. In virtually every case, the position taken there will indicate to which second coming camp the author subscribes.

In Revelation 4:1, John is called up into Heaven, and many pre-tribulationists contend that ascent is symbolic or pictorial of the rapture of the Church. John's ascent may be "spiritual" (as for most pre-tribulational scholars) or literal (as for some), but in either case, they believe that such a "rapture" is symbolic of the Church's pre-tribulational rapture. (Since the account of the horrors of the tribulation comes after Revelation 4:1, the position argues that John misses it, so therefore, the Church must miss it also.) No commentary suggests such a thing unless the writer is strongly predisposed to dispensational pre-tribulationism and, therefore, sees a rapture of the Church here.

First, the text says nothing about the rapture of the Church. In order for John to represent the Church, the text has to be allegorized, and an extraneous concept must be superimposed on it. Second, the essential rationale for seeing the rapture here is that the theorists have to remove the Church from the earth before the occurrence of the tribulation troubles reported in chapters six through eighteen of Revelation, and they force this verse to serve their purpose because they can find no other. Third, a further rationale for interpreting this verse as depicting the rapture is that as the theorists consistently tell us, the Church is not seen on earth after Revelation 4:1.

Several facts must be considered, however, on that subject. It is true that the Church as *ekklesia* is not specifically mentioned by that name in the following chapters, but the theorists don't tell us that neither is it pictured in Heaven by that name. That is a weighty consideration. If the proof that the Church is not on earth because its name *ekklesia* is not used, neither is it in Heaven because that word is not used of it there either. Thus, according to the logic of the theorists, the Church does not exist anywhere on earth during the period described in Revelation chapters four through twenty-two. The argument, however, proves too much. Using such logic, the Church is nowhere in the universe in the Revelation time-frame since, by the label *ekklesia,* it is used nowhere in the book. In fact, the Church as the entire body of Christ is never seen at all in the entirety of the Book of Revelation if the theorists are right. That is true because, although the word *ekklesia* is used nineteen times in the first three chapters, it is never used of the entire body of Christ but only of local congregations. Therefore, to use the same rationale as the pre-tribulationists, we never see the "Church universal" in the entire book. And consider this astonishing fact: the Church is not seen at her own wedding feast in Revelation 19 because the word *ekklesia* is not used there. Further, what are we to say of the other books in the New Testament (Mark, Luke, John, 2 Timothy, Titus, 1 and 2 Peter, 1 and 2 John, and Jude) which do not mention the Church as *ekklesia?* Where, precisely, is the *ekklesia* in those contexts? And what shall we do with a people on earth in the tribulation known as "fellow servants [of the tribulation martyrs] and their brethren" (Revelation 6:11), "servants of our God" (7:3), "saints" (8:3, 13:7, and so forth), "the ones who come out of the great tribulation, and washed their robes and made them white in the blood of the lamb" (7:14), "my two witnesses" (11:3), "the rest of her [the woman's] offspring who keep the commandments of God and have the testimony of Jesus Christ" (12:17), "the redeemed" (14:3–4), those who "follow the Lamb wherever He goes" (14:4), those who "were redeemed from among men, being firstfruits to God and to the Lamb" (14:4), "those who keep the commandments of God and the faith of Jesus" (14:12), "prophets" (16:6), "those who are with [Christ] are called, chosen, and faithful" (16:14), and "my people" (18:4)? Are we to think that not a single one of these refer to the Church? A unified "no" emanates from the pre-tribulationist position. "Not a single one of them is a true Christian in the New Testament sense of the word," is generally the response given.

There are other problems with the text for the pre-tribulationist. John's perspective often changes in the course of the book. It is not always easy to ascertain with definite certainty his location, but we know, for instance, that in Revelation 10:8 (in the "little book" episode) John is commanded to take the book and to give it to the angel who "stands on the earth and the sea." Therefore, John is on earth at this point. We further know that John obeys the command. In 11:1f, he views things from Heaven. In 13:1f, he is back on earth. In 14:1f, he is on Mount Zion which is on earth. In 17:3, he is in the "wilderness." In 18:1f, he is apparently back on earth. And in 22:1, he is in Heaven again. If John represents the Church, then consistency demands that we speculate a series of raptures and "unraptures" for the Church.

Remember, too, that in Revelation 4:1, Jesus does not descend to the earth, does not come down at all, but rather John ascends to Him who does not descend to earth or even toward earth, which is not the pattern of the rapture.

It is commonly stated by pre-tribulationists that John's call to "come up here" symbolizes the rapture of the Church. Interestingly, their best-known proponents deny that view even though they generally believe the rapture occurs at or near the break between chapters three and four of the Revelation. They are forced to that conclusion, again, not by scriptural statements but by the necessity of removing the Church from the earth before the tribulational troubles.

Timothy LaHaye states that John's experience in 4:1 does not teach a pre-tribulational rapture, and his position is the predominant one among leading pre-tribulationists. Even Hal Lindsey does not, to the author's knowledge, specifically state anywhere in his extensive writings that John's experience represents the rapture of the Church. In fact, in his *There's a New World Coming,* which is his commentary on the entire Book of Revelation, no such intimation is given at Revelation 4:1 or elsewhere.[11]

Obviously, if the aforementioned ardent pre-tribulationists will not use Revelation 4:1 to espouse a pre-tribulational rapture of the Church or a rapture of the Church at any time, they must not find it there, and neither should other pre-tribulationists. Furthermore, it goes without saying, again, that no classic commentary in Christian history has ever held that the passage speaks of a pre-tribulational rapture.

Revelation 5:8

"Now when He had taken the scroll, the four living creatures and the twenty-four elders fell down before the Lamb, each having a harp, and golden bowls full of incense, which are the prayers of the saints."

Revelation 5:8 is another favorite of the modern theorists who argue that the twenty-four elders represent the Church as well. In fact, some would put it at the top of any short list of New Testament passages "proving" the doctrine. H. A. Ironside, representing the position of many pre-tribulationists, does hold that the rapture of the apostle John is a symbol of the rapture of the Church. To him and almost all pre-tribulationists, if John represents the Church being raptured, the elders represent the raptured Church worshipping in Heaven, and their being in Heaven before the tribulation events of Revelation chapters six through eighteen, again, demonstrates conclusively that the Church is no longer on earth. Or so say the theorists.

The following statement appearing in the Scofield Bible may be taken as representative of pre-tribulationists: "The appearance of these elders, already glorified, crowned, and enthroned before the opening of the sealed book of judgment (Revelation chapter 5) and before the end-time judgments are loosed upon the world (chapters 6–18), that the Church is not to be subjected to the judicial wrath and judgments of that time (cp. John 5:24, Romans 5:9; 1 Thessalonians 1:10, 5:1–11; Revelation 3:10)."[12]

Since the text says nothing about a rapture of any sort for believers, we are confronted with a serious conundrum. How can John represent the rapture of the Church and find, upon arriving in Heaven, that the Church has already been raptured and is reigning with Christ on high? Further, if believers already have crowns and crowns represent rewards for faithful service to Christ (as pre-tribulationists aver), it means that the judgment has already occurred. When could such a judgment have taken place since they had just arrived? Or do they precede John, making John's rapture-symbolism unnecessary?

A misinterpretation of their song recorded in Revelation 5:9–10 is necessary in any attempt to identify these elders as the Church. Modern translations and notes in many King James Bibles as well indicate that their song is in the third person, not the second. It isn't "us" that God has redeemed but "them"; therefore, the elders cannot represent the Church raptured because the redeemed would certainly sing of "our" redemption, not "theirs." Even the editors of the Scofield Bible translate the verses in the third person, and Darby himself, the famed pre-tribulationist, admitted the mistranslation.

Walvoord, too, acknowledges that modern textual studies indicate that the King James Version is wrong, but he is very hesitant to employ the proper changes in the text because they would militate against a pre-tribulational rapture of the Church. He says, for instance, "If the King James Version is correct..." and "Inasmuch as there is division among scholars as to which version is correct." However, again the vast majority of standard commentaries are in agreement that the KJV was mistaken in its translation of this verse from the original texts. According to Walvoord, if we admit the foregoing (but no serious Greek scholar does), "The evidence is somewhat weighted in favor of considering the twenty-four elders as representative of the Church, and if so, it would be an indication of a pre-tribulational Rapture..."[13] Such is the gravitas of the supposed New Testament bases for pre-tribulationism.

Walvoord says that all the post-tribulationist can do with this passage is to ask questions about it since post-tribulationism cannot be proven with it, but that misses the entire point. The facts are that this verse does not prove either post-tribulationalism or pre-tribulationalism. The post-tribulationist does need this verse to demonstrate the truth of his position, and therefore, he does not use it in any discussion of the subject, and since the elders cannot be used to prove pre-tribulationism, they should be given up as such a "proof."

A huge dilemma for the pre-tribulationists' interpretation is a pressing question. If the elders represent the Church, why are there twenty-four of them? The ancient church believed, almost uniformly, that they represented the entire people of God, both Old Testament saints (under the rubric of the twelve tribes of Israel) and New Testament saints (under the rubric of the twelve apostles), as is seen in Revelation 21:12–14 where the twelve gates represent the twelve tribes of Israel and the twelve foundations represent the twelve apostles, and they, in total, clearly depict the entire redeemed people of God.

The twenty-four elders, then, also represent the entire people of God, heretofore scattered throughout the earth and ages but are now in fulfillment of His eternal promise together praising God in His eternity. However, pre-tribulationists know, as we have seen, that the Old Testament explicitly depicts the resurrection of Old Testament saints after the tribulation and not before (Daniel 12:1–2; Isaiah 24–25; and Isaiah 25:6–12).

This problem has forced some, despite abundant and explicit Old Testament materials, to posit an Old Testament people-of-God resurrection *before* the "time of Jacob's troubles" or, in other words, before the tribulation centering on the Jewish people. This has been done in order to preserve their unique interpretation of this verse, an interpretation unknown for over eighteen centuries in church history. Other pre-tribulationists are simply silent in the face of the glaring inconsistency, or they say that for the first and last time in all of human history, the number twenty-four somehow, though inexplicably, refers to the Church.

The crowns (the lexical form is *stephanos*) of the elders are variously interpreted, but no matter what meaning we attach to them, they do not require a pre-tribulation rapture, an identity of the elders with the Church, or a "works-judgment" and "works-reward" for the Church.

The *Liberty Bible Commentary* offers a full defense of the "elders equals Church" position. The author says on Revelation 4:4: "As important as 3:10 is for the pre-tribulation Rapture, so is this crucial verse. In fact, it is decisive in the matter. How so when it speaks only of four and twenty elders and four and twenty seats?"[14]

The author cites as his support the fact that the elders are enthroned (cf. 3:21). But how does that, in and of itself, contribute to a pre-tribulational rapture understanding? Maybe, as the Church historically held, it is a prediction of God's people—saved Jews and Gentiles—before God's throne. The author also surmises that their number is important. The Levitical priesthood had twenty-four courses (shifts) in Israel (cf. 1 Chronicles 24:7–19). The Church is a priesthood (cf. 1 Peter 2:5–9; Revelation 1:6).

But if this has only to do with the Church, why twenty-four New Testament priests? Where is that number ever used in the Bible in a Church connection? He also emphasizes that their office is indicative; it is an eldership, a representative office, showing that they are not to be understood in an individual capacity (cf. Acts 15:2 and Acts 20:17). Again, one wonders, what possible connection does that have to do with a pre-tribulational rapture? In addition, he believes that their testimony is distinctive (cf. 5:9–10) which would be true only of the Church. Nevertheless, all believers have a "distinctive" testimony. And a part of the distinct testimony of the elders is that it is in the third person, revealing that somebody besides them has been redeemed. In truth, the unredeemed devil in Hell could legitimately sing the same song, using the third person. Next, he comments that they display spiritual insight and are acquainted with the counsels of God (Revelation 5:5; Revelation 7:13; John 15:15). But again, how does that in any sense limit their identity to the Church? Could Moses, who was obviously not a church member in the New Testament sense, "display spiritual insight" and be "acquainted with the counsel of God"? The author states that their garments indicate that they have been redeemed (cf. 3:18). But as in Acts 1:10 and John 20:12, angels are often portrayed in the Bible as being dressed in white, yet pre-tribulationists don't say they are redeemed, nor does anybody else. According to the author, as determinative of all these reasons is the fact that the elders are crowned. It is believed that only saints of the Church Age are promised crowns of gold as rewards. Since the elders have already received them, that means the judgment seat of Christ has taken place (2 Corinthians 5:10). Truly, no one can know precisely why these elders are depicted as being crowned, but to say that such a fact demands that we identify them with the Church does not follow. Further, we have the problem here of John, supposedly representing the raptured Church, finding upon his arrival in Heaven that the Church has already been raptured so much earlier than he that their reward ceremony has already occurred. Which is it then-John or the elder—who represent the raptured Church? And, significantly, why is John not wearing his golden crown?[15]

Although some pre-tribulationists say that the fact that the elders represent the Church is the strongest proof of their position, others in their camp explicitly state that the elders do not represent the Church at all. Noted pre-tribulationist theologian H. C. Thiessen says of the elders:

> There is not sufficient evidence to be certain as to this identification. It is probably as accurate to identify them as some type of heavenly beings such as the seraphim (Isaiah 6:2), cherubim (Ezekiel 10:8), or living creatures (Revelation 4:6), or as some other type of angelic being around the throne of God.[16]

This difference of opinion among the camp itself shows that if one did not come to this passage with a powerful predisposition toward a pre-tribulational rapture, one would never see the twenty four elders, a collective figure never used before or after in a Church connection, as representing a pre-tribulationally resurrected Church.

Who, then, are the elders? Some exegetes see these elders as representing a heavenly council, the patriarchs, the apostles, Old Testament believers, or simply disembodied redeemed spirits in Heaven. The early church almost uniformly saw them as representing the entire people of God, both Old and New Testament.

Reese, after a lengthy discussion listing several possibilities, quoting Bullinger, says:

> 'These four and twenty elders are the princely leaders, rulers, and Governors of Heaven's worship. They are kings and priests. They were not and cannot be the Church of God. They are seen already crowned when the throne is first set up. They are crowned now. They were not and are not redeemed, for they distinguish between themselves and those who are redeemed...They are heavenly, unfallen beings, and therefore they are arrayed in white robes...' In fact, pretty much all recent commentators outside pre-tribs interpret the Elders as leaders in the praise and worship of heaven.[17]

The number of the elders, the Church has always held, represents the totality of the saints, both Old and New Testament believers. The same totality may be seen in the Revelation in the twelve gates of the holy city where we find the names of the twelve tribes and in the twelve foundations of the same city upon which we find the names of the twelve apostles, conjoining in eternal fellowship all the saints of all the ages.

The fact is that we do not know for certain who or what the elders represent, but we do know that the passage should never be used as evidence for any position regarding the timing of the rapture. One has to ponder if an event of such momentous impact as a pre-tribulational deliverance of all the saints of God from the earth were to occur, why would God in contrast to His consistent character and practice not have given His people an explicit statement of such? And why, again, did the elders not represent a pre-tribulationally raptured Church in the entire sweep of Christian history before the modern teaching arose? As we have seen, we search in vain both in church history and in the Bible for such a teaching. There is nothing in this passage that legitimates a pre-tribulational rapture of the Church.

Revelation 3:10

"Because you have kept My command to persevere, I also will keep
you from the hour of trial which shall come upon the whole world,
to test those who dwell on earth."

Revelation 3:10 has to be placed high on any short list of verses which purport to teach a pre-tribulation rapture. Some have placed it at the top of such a list because they believe that it is patently clear that this verse teaches that God is going to rapture the "Philadelphian" church of the future from the world-wide tribulation. Is that true? Can we base our hope or any part of it relating to a pre-tribulation rapture on this verse, or has it, too, been pressed into a service for which it is thoroughly unfitted?

The early church never believed that this verse taught a pre-tribulation rapture. That in itself, again, does not prove the doctrine to be erroneous, but the essential rule of evidence remains to be that the burden of proof is always on the innovator. That is, the older belief must hold sway until it is successfully challenged by the newer belief.

The same language used in this verse is used by the same writer quoting Jesus in John 17:15: "I do not pray that You [God] should take them [the disciples] out of the world [the Greek is *"ares autous ek tou kosmou,"* the precise language that would have been used of a physical rapture], but that you should keep them out of the evil [one] [the Greek is *"all' ina tereses autous ek tou ponerou*]." Jesus' prayer, all are agreed, envisions no physical rapture *away from* but deliverance *through* trouble. Revelation 3:10 states in the Greek *kago se tereso ek tes horas tou peirasmou tes,* meaning, "And I will keep you out of the hour of the trouble." In the gospel passage, we see *tereses ek* and in the Revelation passage we have *tereso ek,* which is precisely the same language by the same author who quotes Jesus in both cases.

This brings us to a critical point. If Jesus' words in John's gospel do not require a physical rapture away from trouble, why do the same words from his mouth in the Revelation demand it? In both places, the promise is protection through the trouble and not deliverance away from it, which has been a common experience of God's people in all generations.

Further, if the deliverance of the sixth of the churches, the Philadelphian church, represents the pre-tribulational rapture of the Church (thus ending the Church Age on earth), how could the seventh church, the Laodicean church, follow it on earth as Revelation 3:14f indicates?

If we hold, as pre-tribulationists do, that the Laodicean church is the apostate church of the last days, it must be remembered that there are promises to those in the church who overcome in the Laodicean church age, and that encouragement would make no sense if there were no legitimate New Testament Church on earth, however carnal. If the Laodicean church, however impure, remains on earth after the Philadelphian rapture, then the view that the Church is not seen on earth during the tribulation is exploded. If the Laodicean church remains on earth following the rapture, it will experience mushrooming growth, the likes of which the world has never seen with multiplied millions entering it. In fact, the numbers coming into its membership will be uncountable (Revelation 7:9). Thus, the dilemma of the pre-tribulationists is this: Laodicea is the death-marked apostate church before the rapture, but it is also the church that will know unprecedented blessing and growth in the seven years immediately following the rapture.

Such inconsistencies represent many other incongruities one runs into attempting to defend the new theory. Again, the situation is not helped by labeling it as "the apostate church of the tribulation"; it is still a church, and it is still on earth, therefore, at least some of its members are surely saved, and all of its members are encouraged to be overcomers. Is the pre-tribulationist prepared to say that not a single soul will be saved in the Laodicean church? And if even one person is saved there, is his salvation in any way different from those saved throughout church history? Is he truly a Christian in the New Testament and even Church Age sense or not? And, parenthetically, are we now in the Laodicean age as we so often hear? If so, why has not the Philadelphian church been raptured?

If the answer is that there is no difference in his salvation and ours, then all is lost because we are told by pre-tribulationists that the "gospel" preached in the tribulation is not the same "gospel" preached during the Church Age. And it is to be remembered that theorists also say that, during the tribulation, the Holy Spirit is not on earth but has raptured away with the Church. It must also be remembered that all this assumes that the seven churches represent "seven church ages," meaning a chronological scheme of the entirety of the Church Age, a view which even some dispensationalists do not hold.

We see in 12:17 (and elsewhere) a people of God in the tribulation period who "keep the commandments of God and have the testimony of Jesus." Are they not Christians? All admit that multiplied millions of Jews and Gentiles will be saved during the tribulation period. Presumably, they will act much like modern Christians. They will repent of their sins, confess Christ, be baptized in Christ's name, construct facilities for their gatherings, meet for worship and instruction, receive offerings, send forth missionaries to preach the gospel across the globe, and so forth. Who can imagine otherwise? What is it, precisely, that prohibits them from being labeled true and genuine Christians belonging to authentic New Testament churches?

In every generation, including our own, in various places around the globe, believers face persecution, even to the death, as they have in every generation. As with His people in Egypt, however, God continues to bless and protect them. Scripture says, "The Lord knows how to deliver the godly out of temptations [2 Peter 2:9; "temptations" is *peirasmou,* which is the same word used in Revelation 3:10]," but He doesn't always do so by means of a physical rapture. Several translations show "preservation through." Many other scholars agree with that language.

Gundry has an excellent discussion of the text and observes that had the author been speaking of a physical rapture he would have more appropriately used various other Greek words than the one he used, which is *ek,* translated "from" in English. Gundry observes that the word means "out from the midst of," thereby demonstrating that, if this passage speaks of a physical rapture, the Church necessarily has to enter into the tribulation, or "out of the midst of" does not fit a rapture before any trouble sets in, but the entire point of a pre-tribulation rapture is that the Church will not even enter into the tribulation period or experience any part of it.[18]

We also know, of course, of historical precedents (for example, Noah, the Hebrews in Egypt, and Rahab) where God's people have been protected through difficult times and of prophecies of the same sort, notably when Jesus promises such to believers in John seventeen.

Such a view reminds us that the troubles of the tribulation period increase in intensity, and we are not to believe that the full expression of wrath, whether God's or anybody else's, will characterize the entire tribulation period. That is a critical issue. Several exegetes have come to a "pre-wrath" position regarding Jesus' return, believing that He will return somewhere toward the end of the tribulation, or just after it but, in any case, before God's wrath is poured out. Although that is closely akin to historical orthodoxy, the issue becomes, then, at precisely what point in the seven year period does Jesus come to deliver His people?

We are on safe ground if we adhere to strict biblical teaching, for instance, that His coming will come after the tribulation and its attendant cosmological signs. Matthew 24:29 states, "Immediately after the tribulation of those days the sun will be darkened, and the stars will fall from heaven, and the powers of the heavens will be shaken." And then, the next verse says that Jesus will come. Historically, the "shortening of days" phrase was interpreted to mean simply that if the period were not limited to seven years total then the intensity of the final three-and-a-half years would be so severe that nobody would live through it.

But what shall we do with the promise of Revelation 3:10 as to its implications beyond the local Philadelphian church? We may well conclude that it does predict deliverance, a deliverance of keeping Christians safe through the period until the Second Coming of Christ. Even if we say that the deliverance is an actual rapture away from the troubles, such a deliverance could still hold true of Jesus' final coming but not a pre-tribulational rapture since such a deliverance could come at the very end of the tribulational period. We need not again distribute God's wrath with equal intensity all through the seven year period. Some have argued that the ultimate judgments expressed in the seals, trumpets, and bowls could conceivably last for only a very short time.

As to the common claim among modern pre-tribulationists that wrath characterizes the entire period, Scofield, who holds to an intensification of the tribulational troubles, is to be noted here:

> Then follow the series of events called the trumpet judgments. There is a significant thing about these. Divine wrath is mingled with the outworking of human wickedness. Up to this time, all

through the opening of the seals, as they are called, it is simply the unrestrained manifestation of that which is already latent in human nature. Now the Divine wrath is manifested and the distress and anguish become unspeakable. (Revelation 8:9)[19]

It must be remembered that the judgments spoken of in Revelation chapters six through eighteen may well be recapitulational and not successive; that is, with each of the series—the seals, trumpets and bowls—we come to the full expression of wrath with the last event of each of the three groups, so that the last seal, the last trumpet, and last bowl all speak of the final expression of God's wrath.

As a final thought on this point of interest, let us ask: "Was the church at Philadelphia, to whom Jesus wrote, an actual, historical congregation?" The answer, on all sides, would be "Yes." If so, another question arises: "Did Jesus make good on His promise to the historical church at Philadelphia to keep them *ek* (or out of) the hour?" The answer, again, has to be "Yes, of course He did, or else He broke His promise." A further question then necessarily follows: "Did He fulfill His promise to the Philadelphian church by means of a physical rapture?" The answer is obvious that He did not.

Walvoord has an interesting solution to some of the problems this passage presents to pre-tribulationists. He says that the members of the Philadelphian church were not raptured because they died before the tribulation ever came; they were, therefore, delivered by their death.[20] But that gives up all pre-tribulational ground which the passage is supposed to prove! Did God promise a physical rapture or did He not? Did such a rapture happen to them or not? If not, then why is it demanded for a future generation? Walvoord admits about this favorite passage that it "may not be decisively in support of pre-tribulationism."

Whatever troubles the Church was to experience or will endure in the future prior to His Second Coming, Jesus delivered it and will continue to do so, not by means of a physical rapture but by means of seeing the Christians through the period. If we say, on the one hand, that He delivered the historic Philadelphian church by protecting its members through trouble of various sorts and that He must deliver some future "Philadelphian" church by a physical rapture into Heaven, then we cannot be surprised if we are accused of serious inconsistency and see ourselves as spiritualizing the meaning of Scripture. In any case, here again, we look in vain in this passage for any evidence of a pre-tribulation rapture.

2 Thessalonianas 2:1–13

"Now, brethren, concerning the coming of our Lord Jesus Christ and our gathering together to Him, we ask you not to be soon shaken in mind or troubled, either by spirit or by word or by letter, as if from us, as though the day of Christ had come. Let no one deceive you by any means; for that Day will not come unless the falling away comes first, and the man of sin is revealed, the son of perdition, who opposes and exalts himself above all that is called God or that is worshipped, so that he sits as God in the temple of God, showing himself that he is God. Do you remember that when I was still with you I told you these things? And now you know what is restraining, that he may be revealed in his own time. For the mystery of lawlessness is already at work; only He who now restrains will do so until He is taken out of the way. And then the lawless one will be revealed, whom the Lord will consume with the breath of His mouth and destroy with the brightness of His coming. The coming of the lawless one is according to the working of Satan, with all power, signs, and lying wonders, and with all unrighteous deception among those who perish, because they did not receive the love of the truth, that they might be saved. And for this reason God will send them strong delusion, that they should believe the lie, that they all may be condemned who did not believe the truth but had pleasure in unrighteousness. But we are bound to give thanks to God always for you, brethren, beloved by the Lord, because God from the beginning chose you for salvation by the Spirit and belief of the truth."

This passage is one that has suffered many novel interpretations despite the fact that Paul's essential message is straightforward. In the face of the Thessalonians questions regarding Christ's return, he says that the Day of the Lord hasn't occurred yet and will not until two events happen: the "falling away" and the manifestation of the "man of sin." Pre-tribulationists cannot have it that way, of course, because the Church will not, in their view, be on earth during the reign of antichrist (the man of sin).

They, therefore, place the "signless" (and for many "secret") rapture of the Church here, although, obviously, it is not mentioned. Logically, from their viewpoint, it has to occur here, and so they must insert it into the text. But, alas, Paul indicates no such thing precisely because he knew nothing of a pre-tribulation rapture, and if he had known about it, how misleading not to say so and leave eighteen centuries and more believers to grope about in the dark concerning the order of end-time events.

Notwithstanding, the pre-tribulationists say that Paul is not speaking of the rapture here but of the "Second Coming" (actually their third one) seven years later. They say phrases such as "the day of Christ," and "that Day" refers here to His final appearing and not to the rapture. Later pre-tribulationists say that all these "days" are the same, and we can only know which one is spoken of by the context, meaning when the context fits the arbitrarily imposed conditions of the theorists.

Several things are to be said about that suggestion: (a) Again, nobody in the first eighteen centuries and more of Christian history ever promoted such a thing, (b) The one second coming of Jesus has always been known by several terms, all of them referring to the same event, though sometimes from differing perspectives: the *parousia* (coming) of Christ, the *apokalupsis* (unveiling or revelation) of Christ, the *epiphaneia* (appearing) of Christ, "the day of the Lord" (or Christ), or simply "the day," and Paul uses the phrase, "our gathering together to Him" (vs 1), which even the pre-tribulationists admit speaks of the single event of rapture, resurrection, and return. It is the one single Second Coming of which the apostle speaks here.[21] Seeing their dilemma regarding the lack of any reference to a pre-tribulational rapture in this passage, some pre-tribulationists have inserted a peculiar idea which, again, was never thought of in the early church, and very few hold today. They argue that the "falling away" itself is the rapture. How do they arrive at that conclusion?

The word *apostasia* ("falling away") is the term Paul uses here, and the theorists say that it may well infer "our gathering together to Him," which is the rapture. They contend that the terms *apostasia* and *rapture* are synonymous. How is that possible? Our word *apostasy* obviously comes from the word, but the theorists affirm that a secondary meaning is "to stand away from" or "to depart from" and, therefore, could legitimately refer to the physical departure of the saints, which is the rapture.

The problem with such an interpretation is that the word is never so used in the New Testament. In fact, it is used only once in Acts 21:21 and refers there to a religious apostasy, a falling away from the truth. It is also never so used in the entirety of the Septuagint, the Greek translation of the Old Testament which the apostles knew well and quoted. It is never so used in either the common Greek language, the *koine,* or in classic Attic Greek. Nevertheless, although it is never used in such a manner, some pre-tribulationists say it is so used here. On this matter, Gundry concludes: "No wonder, then, that NT lexicons uniformly give *apostasia* the special senses of religious apostasy and political rebellion—BAG (Bauer, Arndt, and Gingrich), Kittel, Cremer, Abbott-Smith, Thayer and others."[22] *Uniformly* is the operative word; it seems that the only people who ever thought otherwise are the theorists.

Some years ago, while ministering in Canada, I was perusing books that a retiring pastor was selling when I spotted a book which sent my pulse racing. It was entitled *Re-thinking the Rapture* by E. Schuyler English in which the author had the distinction, some say, of originating the idea that it is proper to translate *apostasia* in the sense of a physical departure or as the rapture.

English begins his discussion by saying, "We suggest, for prayerful consideration, a deviation from the accepted translation and interpretation of this passage."[23] Notice how, to prove a pre-tribulation rapture, request is sought at the outset to depart from the obvious and plain meaning of words and from eighteen hundred years of faithful exegesis. He then launches into a tortured defense of "*apostasia*-equals-rapture" interpretation by tying it to the Greek verb *aphistemi* (to which the noun *apostasia* is distantly related) which means according to the Greek lexicon "to lead away, to seduce, to go away, depart, avoid, withdraw from." "Have we not based our interpretation [making it mean a religious apostasy] upon what may quite possibly be an inappropriate rendition of the Greek noun [*apostasia*]?" asks English. He continues: "If we are not mistaken, we have here a final answer to the time of the translation of the Church in relation to the Tribulation."[24]

Then, in his excursus, he argues that Tyndale in 1539, translates the word as "a departynge," thereby, gratuitously, making Tyndale to refer to physical departure or the rapture. He concludes that this is no novel idea because it has been known "since the 16th century," meaning he found it in Tyndale.[25] What he actually found was his misinterpretation of Tyndale. In truth, Tyndale clearly never thought the word could so be used. The entire passage in English is an intriguing linguistic convolution and demonstrates the barrenness of the land. Why would God tantalize His children for all these centuries by not having His servant say it plainly: "Of course, by this time, the Church has already been translated?" Even so, if English were right, we still have Paul essentially saying the tautological: "The rapture (gathering together) cannot happen until the rapture [the departure] happens."

Many leading pre-tribulationists say we should not so translate the word. As devout a pre-tribulationist as Charles Ryrie was, he says of the word: "An aggressive and climactic revolt against God which will prepare the way for the appearance of the man of sin." Another pre-tribulationist admits that the possibility of *apostasia* referring to the rapture is "most improbable in the light of the meaning of the term in Biblical Greek."[26] Nevertheless, despite the denials of the legitimacy of equating the word with a physical rapture, some still clutch at it as a "proof" of a pre-tribulational rapture.

Walvoord admits that English's interpretation is "somewhat novel," but that if it is admitted, it "constitutes an explicit statement" that the rapture precedes the Second Coming.[27] Either it is a legitimate interpretation or it is not, but it cannot be both ways—"novel" and yet a legitimate proof of pre-tribulationism. No standard commentary in the history of the Christian church allows such an interpretation. Again, the evidence of the (truly) novel teaching of a pre-tribulational doctrine is evident. Although an immense understatement, Walvoord gets it right: "It [apostasia] is normally considered a reference to doctrinal apostasy."[28] (I do not say English originated the "apostasy equals rapture" idea, but some have so stated.)

The vast majority of pre-tribulational writers have nothing to say about apostasia referring to a rapture, which certainly means they do not think it does. But for some, another scripture verse is twisted and forced to say things it was never thought to say and, thus, is perpetuated into a truly arcane idea which not only violates the plain meaning of Scripture and empties the passage of sense but is repudiated by careful students of every stripe. Sadly, the uninitiated are sent forth saying a passage teaches something which it does not.

Another key pre-tribulationist idea is also associated with this passage and, in fact, derives from it. One commonly hears, "The Bible teaches that the Holy Spirit will be removed from the earth when the rapture occurs." Such a theory is based on the following clause in 2 Thessalonians 2:7: "Only He who now restrains will do so until He is taken out of the way." The "he" is taken to refer to the Holy Spirit.

What shall we say as to that possibility? Neither this passage nor any other teaches such a thing. The identity of the "restrainer" has been taken, historically, to refer to persons or entities as diverse as God, government, the Church, or antichrist. We may speculate endlessly, but nobody can say for sure who or what is envisioned here. The language might not have the idea of something or someone being taken away at all; it literally says "comes— or becomes—out of the midst" and may have the idea of someone or something appearing, becoming obvious and not of anybody or anything leaving in any sense of the word. Such is certainly true of the antichrist; at a certain point, he will "rise up out of the midst of...," and some have taken it to refer to that fact. If we do not know, indeed, may never know until the end, who or what the "restrainer" is, we know one thing for certain: the rapture occurs at the *parousia,* and antichrist's career occurs before the parousia. Thus, the order is antichrist, tribulation, parousia, and then resurrection/rapture of believers.

Another idea which has no basis in fact (or Christian history) should be mentioned here. It is the idea that 144,000 Jewish evangelists will take the gospel to the entire tribulation world and countless millions will be won to Christ through their ministry. The eminent pastor-missionary statesman Dr. Oswald J. Smith, pastor of the famed People's Church of Toronto, Canada, calls the idea "preposterous."

He asks "Do you mean to say that after the Holy Spirit has gone, and we are told that He is to go when the Church goes, do you mean to say that the Jews can accomplish more in some seven years or less, without the help of the Holy Spirit, in the midst of persecution and martyrdom, then we have been able to accomplish in nearly two thousand years, with the Holy Spirit's aid, when it has been easy to be a Christian? Preposterous! Impossible!"[29]

2 Thessalonians 1:4–8

Before leaving 2 Thessalonians, a final passage, popular with pre-tribulationists, presents itself.

> "We boast of you among the churches of God for your patience and faith in all your persecutions and tribulations that you endure, which is manifest evidence of the righteous judgment of God, that you may be counted worthy of the kingdom of God, for which you also suffer; since it is a righteous thing with God to repay with

tribulation those who trouble you, and to give you who are troubled rest with us when the Lord Jesus is revealed from heaven with His mighty angels, in flaming fire taking vengeance on those who do not obey the gospel of our Lord Jesus Christ."

First, notice that the word "tribulation" (*thlipsis* is the lexical form) is used four times in the passage. It is the same word, all are agreed, for the "great tribulation" at the end of history. It should be asked of pre-tribulationists how it is that some Christians were undergoing tribulation when Paul wrote, and yet Christians could not because they are members of the body of Christ, the Church, experience it at the end of history.

The usual answer is: the last one is much greater than the former. To which it must be said that it is different in extent but not necessarily in intensity. What of the countless thousands of martyrs in early Christian history (whose lives George Foxe so carefully recorded) and of the millions since? It has been observed that more Christians died for their faith in the twentieth century than in all the preceding centuries combined.

We have no grounds for believing that the last generation of Christians should be delivered from suffering and death simply because they will be a part of the body of Christ which, in the nature of the case (the theorists say), cannot be subjected to suffering. Christians of every generation bear precisely the same relation to God the Father, God the Son, and God the Holy Spirit, and as we have seen, nothing disqualifies them, any of them, from suffering and even martyrdom. Further, what does it say about the nature of commitment to Christ and His cause that modern Christians are so passionate, indeed, so desperate, not to suffer for Christ and His glory but to be delivered from suffering?

In any case, what does the passage under scrutiny teach? First, it does promise relief from suffering. The troubles of the recipients of the letter are intense. At least four English words are used to illustrate their condition: "persecuted" (vs. 4), "tribulations" (vs. 4), "suffer(ing)" (vs. 5), and "trouble" (vs. 6) Now, let us ask this question: At what point in history are

Christians promised rest from persecutions? When does their deliverance come?

Paul plainly and explicitly tells us that God is going to give them rest "when the Lord Jesus is revealed from heaven with His mighty angels, in flaming fire taking vengeance on those who do not know God, and on those who do not obey the gospel of our Lord Jesus Christ" (2 Thessalonians 1:7–8).

The passage says God is going to do two things at the same time: "repay with tribulation those who trouble you" and "give you who are troubled rest." Put otherwise, grammatically, the "righteous" activity God will engage in speaks of two events: to "repay" evil men and to "give rest" to good men. Now, if Paul does not mean that "rest" comes at the last coming of Christ, words have ceased to mean anything.

How do the theorists handle the problem? Actually, they say, the "rest" comes at the rapture seven years earlier because the Day of the Lord begins with the secret rapture, seen only by Christians, and lasts through the millennium. So, they choose, arbitrarily, to place the "rest" at the pre-tribulational rapture.

Words come to mean nothing at all, and people are taught to hope for a "rest" at a time when it will never occur. The ramification of this teaching is that people will be left to go through the tribulational period without any preparation at all for the intense suffering which it provably foresees. If the doctrine of the theorists were right, Paul would have surely said something like this: "You will rest at the pre-tribulation rapture and not after the tribulation seven years later. Let this be your hope, for you will not enter into any part of the fearful judgments which are to befall the earth."Yet he did not say anything like that. He made it as clear as possible at what point the "rest" would come. It comes when Jesus returns in judgment and not seven years before.

Again, if we let the Scripture stand as written, all is clear, but if we force a man-made grid on it, it is mutilated for our Procrustean bed. (Procrustes is a figure from Greek mythology who was a thief, and worse, after taking his victims' valuables, he tortured them to death by placing them in an iron bed and lopping off the limbs of those who were too long for the bed and stretching the limbs of those that were too short.)

One author, feeling the pinch of the obvious meaning of the passage, says that Paul's real focus here is not relief for believers but the coming righteous judgment of God on unbelievers. This again distorts Paul's obvious teaching in the passage. If this passage does not promise rest to persecuted Christians at Jesus' one Second Coming, at which time He takes vengeance on an unbelieving world, the passage is nonsensical. And that is why the ancient church never saw it the way the theorists do and why all non-pre-tribulationists interpret this passage precisely as the early church did.

Luke 21:36

"Watch therefore, and pray always that you may be counted worthy to escape all these things that will come to pass, and to stand before the Son of Man."

Although this passage, too, is quoted many times as support for a pre-tribulational doctrine, instead of answering questions, this passage raises other dilemmas when ascribing it a pre-tribulation interpretation. For example, since all believers—no matter what their walk with Christ—will be raptured, why pray to be "worthy" of it? To be saved is to be in it automatically. It is Christ's worthiness, not that of the Christian, which gets him into the rapture. The passage makes no sense, then, as a defense of pre-tribulationism.

If "escape" means rapture, then the passage teaches too much for the pre-tribulationist because it promises rapture only to those who are spiritually ready—those who are watching and praying—and yet not to all believers. This "escape" is *ekpheugo,* which means "to flee out of, flee away, to seek safety in flight, to escape." Luke used it (without the prefix *ek*) as recently as in verse twenty-one, in which the word obviously encouraged the local people to flee when Jerusalem was attacked. *Ekpheugo* is also used in Acts 16:27 and 19:16, 1 Thessalonians 5:3, Hebrews 2:3 and 12:25, Romans

2:3, and in 2 Corinthians 11:33, but it is never used anywhere in connection with a pre-tribulational coming of Christ.

The prefix *ek* itself is problematic for pre-tribulationists since it means "out of" or "out of the midst of," which would require first being in the condition—in this case the tribulation—out of which one would be delivered. It is impossible to escape the difficulty concerning how one can be delivered out of something into which that person has never entered. The same holds of *ek* in Revelation 3:10, as we previously noted. If the intent was to communicate that one was being delivered from something without ever being in it, the appropriate preposition would have been *apo,* which means "away from" and not *ek,* which means "out of."

There are other problems for a pre-tribulational use of this passage. First, how is it that up to this point in the passage, the disciples represent the Jews in the tribulation, yet suddenly, they represent the Church? We have jumped from "Jewish ground" to "Church ground" without warning. Second, the tribulation is supposed to be a signless event, but this passage comes in the context of a lengthy discussion of various signs precursive to Jesus' coming: "And there will be signs in the sun, in the moon, and in the stars; and on the earth distress of nations, with perplexity, the sea and the waves roaring" (verse 25); we are given the "fig tree" sign (verse 29), and then in verse thirty-one, we read: "So you also, when you see these things happening, know that the kingdom of God is near."

We are asked to believe, then, that Jesus is saying something like this: "After you see all these signs, you will know that the end is near, not here yet but near. However, you will have already been raptured away, and so when you see the signs, be ready for the pre-tribulational rapture." Gundry says in reference to this discussion:

> Jesus tells his disciples to pray that they might be able 'to escape all these things that are going to happen' [the events of the tribulation] and consequently 'to stand before the Son of man' [whose return has just been described]. In the first place the context has spoken

only about the Son of man's coming after the tribulation (verses 25-27). In the second place, Luke uses the verb 'escape' elsewhere only in Acts 16:27, 19:16, and neither time does it mean avoidance of entrance—rather, exit from within [escaping out of jail in the first instance, out of a house in the second]. So escaping the events of the tribulation hardly means non-entrance in to it; rather, coming out of it with your faith intact so as to enjoy the presence of the returned Christ.[30]

What has been the common interpretation of the passage throughout the centuries? The consensus is that it refers to escaping by means of physical flight from the vortex of trouble in and around Jerusalem and the tribulational events occurring in the area. That makes sense since Luke has been describing tribulational troubles in the context. "Standing" then, refers to preserving one's life until Christ's actual return. Parenthetically, this verse also demonstrates that the suffering of the tribulational period is of varying degrees depending on one's location, which could necessitate running to a safer place.

Interestingly, the word *worthy* is debated. The manuscript evidence is split between two words (*kataksiothete* and *katischusete*), the first having the idea of being morally worthy and the second one having the idea of being physically strong. Either word would make sense in a Second Coming context (maintaining either moral or physical strength in the face of tribulation), but neither would in a pre-tribulational rapture sense because it would imply that moral or physical superiority qualifies one for the rapture, which cannot be true since salvation by God's grace alone accomplishes that.

Matthew 24:40–41

"Then two men will be in the field: one will be taken and the other left. Two women will be grinding at the mill: one will be taken and the other left."

Post-tribulationists see in this verse the post-tribulational rapture, following the just-described tribulational events. Pre-tribulationists, however, say that this passage cannot speak of a post-tribulational rapture because the people who are "taken" go away to judgment and not to the returning Savior while those who are "left" remain on earth to enjoy the blessings of the millennial kingdom, indicating that they are saved.

The passage seems initially to affirm a pre-tribulational rapture with the saved ones going away, not to be judged but to meet the coming Savior and the lost left to experience the Savior's wrath and not the blessings of the millennial kingdom. Several considerations, however, must be taken into account in the interpretation of the passage. This single passage must not be taken as the primary basis or the entire revelation for settling the question as to the timing of the rapture because Jesus used a different word in verses forty and forty-one (*paralambano*) for "taken" than He did in verse thirty-nine when the flood victims were "taken" (*airo*). Surely, He was distinguishing between the two "takings" with one being to judgment and the other to blessing. Also, *paralambano* has in it the idea of close association with the one taken; thus, it fits better with the idea of a rapture—that of being in close association with Christ——than with judgment. The separation between the good and the evil occurs, say pre-tribulationists, not at the rapture but at the sheep and goat judgment which follows, but why separate them there when they have already been separated at a pre-tribulational rapture?

Reese quotes, D. M. Panton on this passage and its parallel in Luke 17:34–35:

> 'With the view that the taken are taken to judgment, and the left are left to glory, it is needless to say more at present than that it is built on a single (not unnatural) misconception. For the word "took," in the case of the Antedeluvians—"*took* them all away"—means "to arrest," "to take to *destruction*"; whereas when "one is *taken* and one is left," the word means "to take *as a companion*." *It is a rapture of honour;* it is the word used when our Lord selects three only out of the Twelve for watchfulness against the great

tribulation of Gethsemane, the select resurrection of Jairus's daughter, and the kingdom glory of the Transfiguration..."*One is taken into safety* and one is *left to his fate*." That gives exactly the sense of the passages,' he says, quoting Wade's translation.[31]

Genesis 19

In any short list of supposed proofs of pre-tribulationism is the experience of Lot recorded in Genesis nineteen. God's judgment befell Sodom only after Lot was removed, and it is said that Lot is a picture of God taking His Church away before wrath falls on the earth.

Some Christians, lay and ordained, employ not explicit statements in Scripture demonstrating a pre-tribulational rapture but various Old Testament stories, such as that of Lot here, which, as we shall see, militates against the very thing it is purported to prove.

First, let it be said that the Bible nowhere says that Lot's experience represents the rapture of the Church. Luke does record that our Lord mentioned Lot in the context of tribulation events, but it was to communicate that, in the days of the end, men would be living precisely as they did in Lot's day—eating, drinking, planting, building—and, therefore, not preparing for His return. Jesus then stated that when the tribulation comes and is so oppressive we should not go back into the house to retrieve material things but flee for our lives. To drive His truth home, He alluded to Lot's wife: "Remember Lot's wife" (Luke 17:32).

Thus, this Old Testament passage is not about a signless rapture of the Church in a pre-tribulational setting but about being ready for tribulational events whenever they come. That is what Lot himself represents—a man prepared for judgment whenever and however it comes.

However, even if Lot does represent the Church being raptured away from tribulational troubles, the text produces serious difficulties for pre-tribulationists. Get the picture in Sodom. Every man in town, the Bible says, was a homosexual, "The men of Sodom, both old and young, all the people from every quarter, surrounded the house..." (Genesis 19:4), and they were demanding sexual relations with angels. Such a civic condition sounds a great deal like the tribulation, does it not? The situation was so severe that Lot offered his own daughters to the citizenry in the place of the visiting angels. Again, such a desperate and decadent situation is expressive of what may well occur in the tribulation.

Furthermore, Jesus said as does the writer of Genesis that on the very day Lot "went out from Sodom it rained fire and brimstone from heaven and destroyed them all" (Luke 17:29). Not seven years later. Not seven days later. On the very same day.

If the passage teaches anything at all about the *timing* of the rapture as it relates to the tribulation, although no reason exists to think it does, it teaches first the rapture and then immediately following the ruin, which is eschatological orthodoxy. And neither, of course, can it legitimately be called "signless."

We must also examine the account of Noah since Luke records in the same context Jesus' use of him regarding preparedness for the Second Coming. Noah, too, is used by pre-tribulationists to demonstrate that God will remove His people before judgment falls. It is patently obvious that God did not physically rapture His followers to Heaven in Noah's day but that He protected them *through* His judgment on earth.

Noah is never used as an illustration of a pre-tribulation rapture; his society is used as an illustration of non-preparedness for God's judgment. In fact, if Noah's experience has anything to say about the coming tribulation in view of the horrific decadence of his society, the message is that God's deliverance was post-tribulational and not pre-tribulational. Scripture says of His world: "Then the Lord saw that the wickedness of man was great in the earth, and that every intent of the thoughts of his heart was only evil continually" (Genesis 6:5). That sounds a great deal like the coming Babylonish society at the end of human history, which the theorists say Christians will never see since they will have been raptured away seven years earlier.

PART THREE

Common Objections

Scrutiny of the Post-tribulational Rapture Position

It is of utmost importance that we observe in any and all discussions of specific biblical texts which purport to teach pre-tribulationism that the leading pre-tribulationist of this generation, Dr. John Walvoord, has written that pre-tribulationists admit that no specific Scripture passage explicitly teaches the doctrine. He contends that one of the problems before both the pre-tribulation and post-tribulation positions is that both points of view are inductions based upon scriptural facts rather than explicit statements made in the Bible.[1] He adds that "adherents of either view usually concede there is no explicit reference."[2]

Such a statement calls for two observations. First, Walvoord's admission relegates every word of Scripture purporting to teach pre-tribulationism to an inference and nothing more and denies any and all claims to the contrary by other pre-tribulationists. Second, post-tribulationists certainly do not "usually concede that there is no explicit reference" to post-tribulationism and, as we shall see, explicitly state their case to the contrary.

With this in mind, aside from the clear and explicit teaching of the foregoing biblical passages, one commonly hears certain objections to the doctrine of a post-tribulational return of Christ. It is a natural thing to attempt to apply logic to all things under discussion, but one must always affirm the biblical witness first. God has commanded us to love Him with all our minds, but He has also told us to trust His revealed word whether it accords with our logic or not. If our faith is not unreasonable, it is certainly in much of its expression above and beyond reason. We shall see, however, that the objections typically fail both tests, that of Scripture as well as that of reason. We turn now to the most common of such objections to post-tribulationism.

1. "Is not post-tribulationalism a new doctrine?"

It is beyond strange that such an objection is ever made in view of the provable historical fact that the doctrine has been taught since the days of Christ and the apostles and that nobody ever promoted the pre-tribulational scheme until the early nineteenth century. Because one has never heard of it before does not mean that it is "new" any more than the doctrine of the blood atonement is "new" when an unbeliever first hears it.

The demonstrable fact is that Christian history is almost 2000 years old, and the doctrine of a pre-tribulation rapture is only approximately 170 years old. That does not make it right or wrong; it should, however, forever settle the "new-old" question.

2. If the tribulation occurs before Jesus comes, then Christians are not looking for Christ but the antichrist.

First, how is it that the first eighteen centuries of Christians saw no problem with anticipating the antichrist while looking for the Savior? What was their blessed hope? Why did they never see any disparity or difficulty in believing they would experience tribulation (and antichrist) and yet could still legitimately look forward with immense joy to Christ's return?

How could Barnabas, writing before 100 AD, say, "The final stumbling block [or source of danger] approaches...for the whole [past] time of your faith will profit you nothing, unless now in this wicked time we also withstand coming sources of danger...That the Black One (Antichrist) may find no means of entrance..."[3] And how could Augustine, even though an a-millennialist, say: "But he who reads this passage [Daniel 12], even half asleep, cannot fail to see that the kingdom of Antichrist shall fiercely, though for a short time, assail the *Church...*"⁴ The characteristic mood of the church fathers was to look rejoicingly for the coming of Christ to judge wicked men and to bless His Church after a period of intense persecution by antichrist.

Scripture clearly tells us to anticipate the antichrist before Christ's appearing. John says, "Little children, it is the last hour; and as you have heard that the Antichrist is coming, even now many antichrists have come, by which we know that it is the last hour" (1 John 2:18).

Why does John encourage Christians to anticipate the antichrist's coming if indeed Christians won't be on earth when he comes? And how can Paul meaningfully warn Christians that antichrist must come before "our gathering together unto Him" (2 Thessalonians 2:3–8) if we're not to anticipate the coming of antichrist? And how can Peter explicitly state that all Christians should be "looking for and hastening the coming of the Day of God" (which occurs, all admit, at the end of the antichrist's career), "because of which the heavens will melt with fervent heat" (2 Peter 3:2), if in fact all Christians will be raptured seven years earlier?

Peter's exhortation simply doesn't make sense from the theorist's point of view. Why be told to look for something which, in the nature of the case, we could never see anyway? "Looking for" means looking for! And in the following verse, he says we are looking for something else as well, "a new heaven and a new earth in which dwelleth righteousness." When does that occur? Only after antichrist has been defeated according to Revelation 21:1. So, what does Peter, like John and Paul, tell us? That we should be looking for Christ? Yes, but we are to look for Him beyond the tribulation events which must occur first. In fact, it could be argued that nobody looks for the Second Coming of Christ today with anything like the intensity that will characterize Christians at the end of the tribulation.

Many modern Christians, mired in materialism and immorality, rarely if ever think about Christ's return. In fact, many segments of the Church do not even believe it is to be a literal event. It will be a different story at the end when the Church will be fairly sighing and crying for Jesus to return, singing, "Hope of all our hopes the sum; come and take thy waiting people home."[5] Today the issue is a dilettantish discussion, but then it will be a desperately desired deliverance. It must be added, in a precise sense, that which we look for is not deliverance from suffering. Our great hope is union with the resplendent Christ, who is our very life, when He returns in glory.

3. If we cannot believe in an any moment rapture, what does that do to the New Testament doctrine of "imminence"? Can Christ come at any time or can He not? And if certain events were predicted to occur before His return, have they not all occurred, so that now Jesus can come at any moment?

To say that Jesus can come at any moment now because all the required signs have been fulfilled is to deny the very heart of pre-tribulational imminence. Remember that those who believe the doctrine teach that, following Jesus' ascension, He could have come at any moment thereafter without a single sign preceding His coming. The doctrine, so deeply cherished and widely propogated, cannot be rewritten at this late stage.

Some pre-tribulationists, admitting the explicit promises of intervening events, say that all such predicted events could have occurred in the lifetimes of the apostles. Not only is that not true, it totally gives away their doctrine. The apostles, if that were so, could never have taught or written "any-momentism." Either He could have returned *any moment* after the ascension or the teaching is voided. Further, all the predicted signs or precursors of His return have not yet occurred. Paul explicitly tells us that the falling away and the appearance of antichrist must happen before Jesus returns.

The answer then is that the early church believed in imminence if by the word one means that Jesus would come following certain events. If that is not what is understood by the word "imminence," then the New Testament does not teach imminence. Neither in the New Testament nor in the church fathers—the students of the apostles—is such a doctrine found.

Again, it is true that the fathers often spoke of Christ's soon coming, but it was because they felt they were already in the beginning days of the tribulation. In that context, yes, they thought, Jesus might return at any time. (And that was largely true, as many pre-tribulationists state, of the Reformers.) In any case and in every case, the fathers (if they addressed the issue at all) uniformly believed the Church would be on earth during the time of antichrist.

Sometimes, it is said that the pre-tribulational truth was lost like the doctrine of salvation by grace and then later, as with the doctrine of grace, was recovered. The fact is that pre-tribulationism was never taught, either by the Bible or by anybody else, and salvation by grace is taught on almost every page of the epistolary New Testament, and the doctrine of salvation by grace has never been totally lost since apostolic days.

Other such "lost" doctrines are reputed to be those of the Trinity and of human depravity. In fact, depravity is explicitly taught, again, throughout the New Testament (and explicitly so in the early church fathers), and the Trinity, while never being systematically taught in the Bible, was nevertheless recognized as a cardinal truth during the earliest days of the Christian faith.[6]

The doctrine of the Trinity was not lost and then found. The same holds true of all the doctrines of the New Testament. No New Testament doctrine can be named which was totally "lost and then recovered." Even if so, the teaching of a pre-tribulational rapture (with or without all the attendant "dispensational" themes) was completely unknown for the first eighteen centuries of church history.

The matter of "imminence" is monumentally important to the pre-tribulationists. In fact, they themselves admit that the doctrine of pre-tribulationism stands or falls with the doctrine of imminence. Many pre-tribulationalist writers have so stated, and would agree with Walvoord: "For all practical purposes the abandonment of the pre-tribulational return of Christ is tantamount to abandonment of the hope of His imminent return."[7]

The New Testament, however, abounds in passages which demonstrate conclusively that Christ could not have come at any moment after His ascension. For example, Jesus clearly told Peter that he would grow old and die
(John 21:18–19). Peter died in the late 60s AD, some thirty years after
Jesus' prediction. For Peter to write, therefore, that Jesus could have come
at any time following His ascension would have been a blatant inconsistency. And, of course, had he believed in "any-momentism" he could never
have written 2 Peter 3:10–13 in which he bids us to look not to a rapture
but to the tribulation.

Some pre-tribulationists label such observations as being "trivial" or "incon-
sequential"; in fact, the observations are unanswerable.

One pre-tribulation author, attempting to explain the obvious conflict
between an any-moment return of Jesus and Jesus' prophecy of Peter's old age
and death (John 21), says the apostle was well past middle life when the death
prophecy was given and that the prophecy was "apparently not common property of the Church" until after Peter died, and therefore, for most Christians,
this poses no obstacle in believing the imminency of the Lord's coming.[8]

Such a position clearly does not solve the problem. Did Peter know or did he
not know that an any-moment doctrine of Jesus' return was impossible in
view of the death prophecy? To put it another way: does the number of people who know a doctrine have anything to do with its truthfulness? Further,
knowing the impossibility of an any-moment return of Christ, why did he not
correct such a view if such was being espoused by other Christians? And how
could he, one of the two leading spokesmen (along with Paul) of the faith,
more than three decades later, write his second epistle espousing an any-
moment return (as we are told he did) when he knew, from the Lord's own
lips that such a doctrine could not possibly be true? We are, in fact, being
asked to believe that Simon Peter knew the truth but willfully hid it for perhaps the better part of four decades. The writer did not deal with other problems in regard to Peter: the fact that nowhere in any of his writings did Peter
say a syllable indicating "any-momentism" and the fact that, again, Peter, in

harmony with all the other apostles, warned all Christians to be prepared for the Day of the Lord, a day of judgment on the earth.

In the "Olivet Discourse" of Matthew twenty-four, Jesus explicitly predicts the fall of Jerusalem in 70 AD. How then could He have returned before then? That means that Jesus knew He could not return for at least another thirty-seven years or so after giving the discourse. In Matthew 24:8, Jesus said that, even in the light of "wars and rumors of wars" that "the end is not yet," following a prediction in the last times of "famines, pestilences, and earthquakes in various places" and that "all these are the beginning of sorrows." After encouraging Christians to be faithful witnesses through horrible times, He promises that many false prophets would arise and that "the love of many shall grow cold." He says in verse thirteen, "But he that endures to the end shall be saved." He follows that with verse fourteen: "And this gospel of the kingdom will be preached in all the world as a witness to all the nations, and then [and only then] will the end come." One searches in vain in the entire passage for "any-momentism" but sees the precise opposite—much must occur before Christ's return.

The "Great Commission" (Matthew 28:19-20), which commands Christians to take the gospel to all the earth, to make disciples, to mark disciples (with baptism), and then to mature disciples becomes a farce if Jesus did not envision some length of time to intervene between His death and His return. And, significantly, Jesus promises to be with His disciples "until the end of the age," a term which, all admit, stretches to His final return in glory.

If, as many pre-tribulationists hold, the seven churches of Revelation two and three represent seven church ages, how could Jesus have come, say, between churches number two and number three? The Scofield Bible says that church number two, Smyrna, represents the Church under persecution from about AD 100 to AD 316 and that church number three, Pergamum, represents the Church during the Middle Ages, perhaps up until the Reformation.[9] The theory of the seven churches representing seven church ages, which is held by the great majority of pre-tribulationists, alone gives the patent false assertion to an any-moment return of Christ. Either the "church ages" will run their course, or Jesus can come at any moment, but both things cannot occur.

The Holy Spirit warned Paul through the prophet Agabus that troubles would befall him if he went to Jerusalem: "And as we stayed many days, a certain prophet named Agabus came down to Judea. When he had come to us, he took Paul's belt, bound his own hands and feet, and said, 'Thus says the Holy Spirit, "So shall the Jews at Jerusalem bind the man who owns this belt, and deliver him into the hands of the Gentiles"'" (Acts 21:11). The simple question then becomes: did the Holy Spirit know or did He not know that Jesus could not return before the occurrence of the events He predicted through Agabus?

God knew, it must be admitted, that the prophesied events would take place. It will not do to say cavalierly, "Well, that all was to happen in a matter of a few days." Yes, but the point is that it was to happen after it was stated, and for Jesus to have returned before it occurred would be to open Himself to the justifiably charge of either lying or not knowing the future. In fact, all genuine prophecy is impossible if Jesus could have come at any moment following His ascension.

Sometimes pre-tribulationists, attempting to superimpose their "immenency" over such prophecies, say that the predictions were conditional; that is, they might have come to pass and they might not have come to pass. Not only is that not true but taken to the extreme, such a position eviscerates all genuine prophecy.

Earlier, God told Paul that He would deliver him "from the Jewish people, as well as from the Gentiles, to whom I now send you" in a lifetime of missionary service (Acts 26:17). Is it possible that God's prophecy could not have come true? That He would send His Son before His promises to Paul came true? The answer is, of course, "Impossible!" Later, in Acts 27:24, God promised that Paul "must be brought before Caesar." Paul, therefore, obviously could never have taught "any-momentism." At the very least, Paul would have professed something of the following: "I don't know exactly when Christ is coming back, but I know for certain that I will speak to Caesar before He does. I have God's personal word on that." Again, the various promises Christ made cannot be said to be conditional; He predicted certain events which would infallibly come to pass, and He did so, among other reasons, to demonstrate His omniscience, which would have predictably been called into question had those events not occurred.

The Book of Revelation, most are agreed, was written in the late nineties AD, perhaps 96 or 97. In Revelation 10:11, after the episode of eating the "little book," John is informed by God, "You must prophesy again about many peoples, nations, tongues, and kings." In giving that prophecy, the omniscient God knew that John would live at least long enough to utter God's message even if that only meant finishing the Book of Revelation, and therefore, God could never have inspired anybody to teach "any-momentism" before the mid-nineties AD at the earliest.

In view of the fact that the Book of Revelation is the last New Testament book to have been written, that means that no writer of a single New Testament book could have been inspired by God to teach an any-moment imminence. It is simply impossible without devastating theological results as the discovery that God is capable of lying or, at the very least, of being limited in His knowledge as the modern heresy called "open theism" teaches.

One single historic fact demonstrates conclusively and unanswerably why Jesus could not have returned before the mid-twentieth century. Daniel's seventieth week, the tribulation period, begins when antichrist signs a covenant (or "causes a covenant to prevail") with Israel. At that moment, to use the language of the pre-tribulationist, "God's time-piece begins to tick again," meaning that, since the end of the sixty-ninth week, a hiatus (which Daniel did in fact predict) of almost 2000 years has existed in which "God is dealing with the Church, not Israel." But, they say, at the beginning of the tribulation period, God begins to "deal with the Jew again."

Herein lays the problem. Such a covenant could not possibly have been signed with and by Israel before the nation of Israel existed. The historical necessities are obvious. Israel must exist as a nation, antichrist must arise, and immense troubles must engulf the nation before such a covenant could happen. And Israel, obviously, did not become a nation until May 14, 1948. It is futile to say that "it could have happened earlier." First, in any case, a certain amount of time would have been necessary, and second, God Himself knew from eternity past precisely how much time it would take with the result that He could never, therefore, have inspired any of His servants to teach an any-moment rapture.

4. If we give up the idea that Jesus might return at any moment, will that not cut the nerve of evangelism?

Fifty pages could well be spent answering this objection, but Christ's true followers will only need a single sentence: "When will Jesus' straightforward command to tell others about Him be enough to produce proper, persistent, and passionate evangelistic activity?"

Consider two other matters: (a) What is it that inspired the world-mission movement before anybody on earth ever heard about pre-tribulationism? (b) Jesus Himself said that only after the gospel has been preached to the entire world would He return. It can be cogently argued then that pre-tribulationism itself cuts the nerve of evangelism because, as its adherents teach, the mythical 144,000 Jewish evangelists are going to accomplish that task. If so, in the light of their coming success, it might be said that the work of the modern church has been a spectacular failure. In fact, Dr. Oswald J. Smith argues that very point:

> I know of no heresy that can do more to cut the nerve of missionary endeavor [than that of a supposed 144,000 Jews evangelizing the world.] Moreover, I know of no definite statement in the entire Bible that would lead me to believe, for one single moment, that the Jews are to evangelize the world during the days of the great

tribulation, as some people seem to think. Were I to believe that I would fold my arms and do nothing.[10]

5. On the subject of evangelism, despite what Dr. Smith said, is it not provably true that pre-tribulationists are more effective at soul-winning because of their "any-moment" view of the Second Coming?

Obviously, we have no way of knowing by statistical analysis, which eschatological systems have produced more true converts than others. Every true Christian, no matter what his theological beliefs, ought to be passionate and persistent in telling forth the blessed evangel. To quote Moses, "Oh, that all the LORD'S people were prophets and that the LORD would put His Spirit upon them!" (Numbers 11:29), and assuredly, Moses could have added, "And may it happen before any one of them comes to a perfect perception of what God will do about end-time events."

Let the following facts be admitted by all: (a) God knows how to bring to Himself whom He will, and He knows the best means of doing so. (b) He will bring men to Himself by means of His truth without it having to be manipulated, in any way by anybody, to make it "more effective." (c) It is impossible as Jesus told us in His "wheat and tares" parable to accurately define "effectiveness" in evangelism before we get to Heaven. What appears to be most "effective" now will, far too often for our joy, be proven not to be effective in God's eyes.

Further, worst things than being ineffective may befall us, things such as being guilty of superimposing a man-made system onto the Word of God in an attempt to render it more effective. Only one philosophical movement originated in America, that of "pragmatism" or "utilitarianism." The philosophy says, "Whatever works is true. Whatever is effective is to be accepted and followed." If it has, as pragmatists are wont to say, "cash value," then it must be our guide. That philosophy permeates western culture, and some would argue that it is an insidious disease which is rampant and widespread in the American church, too, producing disastrous effects.

Aside from the question of effect, though, to superimpose a philosophical system onto God's Word is much worse than "gilding the lily"; it is to engage in the sheerest form of idolatry. It is to assume one is wiser than God, that one knows better how to draw men to Christ than the Holy Spirit does. Scripture says that Christians are born again by "the word of God which lives and abides forever" (1 Peter 1:23), not by God's Word being distorted and manipulated by even the most well-meaning men. All church plans and methodologies and processes and programs must be judged by God's revelation and not vice versa.

The God-ordained way of evangelism is clearly stated in 2 Corinthians 4:2: "But we have renounced the hidden things of shame, not walking in craftiness nor handling the word of God deceitfully, but by manifestation of the truth commending ourselves to every man's conscience in the sight of God." That evangelism, the one which "manifests the truth," as is surely admitted and affirmed by all sincere Christians, will prove to be the most truly effective in God's eyes.

The question then, about all systems of theology, is not "What works?" but "What has God said?" Lines from the famed German philosopher and poet, Theodor Storm (1817–1888), come to mind:

> One man may ask, 'What comes of it?'
> Another, 'What is right?'
> And that is what distinguishes
> The vassal from the knight.[11]

6. Surely no one would wish the tribulation on anybody, much less fellow Christians.

Surely! But that is not the issue. Wishes do not always square with reality. "If wishes were horses, beggars would ride," but in the real world, wishes are not horses, and so beggars still walk.

One well-known pre-tribulationist author asks it something like this: "Can you look at your precious child and know for certain that she will not suffer at the hands of the antichrist?" First, that is an expression of quintessential American Christianity: "If it's painful, it must not be the will of God. Anything for you, dear Lord, but suffering. Let the poor miscreants, the 'tribulation saints,' be slain by the hundreds of millions; that's their trouble and not mine."

What shall we say of those scores of millions of Christians who have died as martyrs to the faith? (A sobering book, one which ought to be required reading for all new Christians, is the celebrated *Foxe's Book of Martyrs,* which catalogues, in eight volumes in the original, the sufferings and, in many cases, the martyrdom, of countless thousands of early Christians.) And what of the very apostles themselves, all of whom died, tradition says, martyrs' deaths? And what of the tens of thousands of Christians who lost their property, who were forced to see their children hacked to pieces, and who were then made to watch while men raped their wives before being beheaded under the brutal reign of Idi Amin in Uganda? And what of the millions of third-world Christians being threatened with martyrdom and dying as result of persecution during our day?[12]

Theirs is an unimaginable horror—entire Christian villages being wiped out, men being tortured to death, women having their breasts burned off, their pregnant Christian sisters having their unborn babies ripped from their bodies, younger girls being sold for a pittance or a favor into a lifetime of sexual slavery. Are they not true Christians, as much a part of the body of Christ as any other Christian? Consider how we are told by missiologists that more Christians have been martyred for their faith in the twentieth century than in all the previous centuries since Jesus was here. What about such martyrs? Were they members of Christ's body or not?

Because such suffering is not worldwide, we are told that it "is not as bad as the coming tribulation; therefore, such suffering is not relevant to the discussion." But these Christians are a part of the blood-bought body of Christ. And if so, it cannot be argued, "God would never allow His blood-purchased children, the precious Bride of His son, to suffer martyrdom."

Are we to believe that it is ethical for God to allow some of His children to suffer and die today, but it is not ethical for Him to allow others of His children to suffer and die tomorrow?

To say such a thing, all thoughtful persons would readily admit, demonstrates a distorted logic, not to mention a denial of clear biblical teaching. In fact, such suffering is different from what will occur in the great tribulation only in quantity but not in quality.

The Bible-taught Christian says something like this: "Dear God, I do not know what my life of faithfulness to You will bring me or mine, whether pain or pleasure, but I know this: You will give me grace, one way or the other, to honor You and to remain true to You to the end." That, by the way, is a short version of the message of the entire Book of Revelation.

7.   How could so many sincere people be so wrong about it?

How can any sincere and studious Christian be wrong about anything? Why could Peter and Paul have differed so as is reported in Galatians chapter two? How could the differences between Paul and John Mark have become so contentious that a fellowship crisis in that early missionary team was produced? How can there be so many diverse denominations today? How can two Christian luminaries such as John Calvin and John Wesley differ so radically about how God saves men, one being "Calvinist" and the other "Arminian"? Christians differ. In any case, it is essential, however, to remember that pre-tribulationism is not the doctrine of the early church, no matter how many sincere people believe the teaching today.

The apostles and the disciples of the apostles—the church fathers—knew nothing about it, and the pre-tribulational view is, even by the admission of its proponents, the minority view today. Nevertheless, whatever the numbers, God does not establish truth by majority vote. As every Bible student knows, the Bible is full of stories in which the minority was right and the majority was wrong and vice-versa.

8. The two events, the rapture and the revelation, sound so different that they must be two different events.

Much is made of that supposition, but it is, as the attorneys say, "a distinction without a difference."

To begin with, again, it must be asked: why did all that supposed incongruity escape the close scrutiny of Bible students for eighteen hundred years? I know we have asked that question several times throughout this book, but it is a substantive one, and one with which all people seeking truth must come to terms. Why would God take away all joy in the Second Coming of Christ (if the new theory is correct) from His Church for over eighteen hundred years? And how is it that the largest portion of the Church on earth today is totally deprived of a proper joy in regard to the Lord's return because they are so benighted as to look forward—*through the tribulation events*—to that return?

Pre-tribulationists are notorious for their ability to distinguish the two events, the pre-tribulation return of Jesus and the end-time return of Jesus seven years later. In fact, what is akin to desperation marks the attempt to prove the total irreconcilability of the two events. If the events are not essentially disparate, fundamentally different and provably incompatible, all is lost for the theory.

In any study of the issue, several things must be kept in mind: (a) Again, for over eighteen hundred years nobody saw the disparity. (b) Many of the so-called differences which various authors cited have no relationship at all to the specific issue of the great tribulation; they deal with other contexts. (c) Almost always, the supposed incompatibilities exist only if one comes to the issue with a pre-tribulational bias to begin with because apart from such an assumption no problem exists with collating all of the various aspects of the event into one single event as was done by the early church. (d) Additionally, many of the claimed "incompatibilities" perceived of post-tribulationalism are not incompatible at all.

For instance, there is no incompatibility in Christ coming "for" His Church and "with" His Church in the same time frame, nor is there any problem with Christ coming "in the air" and to the earth in the same trip. (Some older pre-tribulationists were wont to say that He comes *to* the air or *into* the air, but the Bible never says such. In fact, it affirms, clearly, that He comes *in* the air.)

The day can be, despite the theorists' contentions, both a day of blessing and a day of judgment as is prophesied in both testaments. If we ask, "Is it not true that signs do not precede the rapture and signs do precede the revelation," the answer is yes; it is true if we arbitrarily say so because of a preconceived bias but no if we do not. There is no biblical problem with the marriage supper of the Lamb and the judgment supper occurring at or near the same time. The resurrection of Old Testament saints can, indeed, occur at the same time as the resurrection of Christians—precisely as we are told in 1 Corinthians 15:54–55 (as Paul quotes Isaiah 25:8, proving a post-tribulational resurrection for the Old Testament saints). Both events are visible, despite the contention that the rapture is seen only by the Church.

One of the writers cited says that an essential difference between the two events is that Christ comes in the rapture as "the bright and morning star" (Revelation 22:16), but in the revelation as "the sun of righteousness...with healing in His wings" (Malachi 4:2). Jesus has over two hundred names in Scripture; does each name describe another coming? Why not change the order of the names and say that He comes in the rapture as the "star" and at the revelation as the "sun" since the names are arbitrarily assigned to the two events? The "bright and morning star" passage in Revelation 22:16 has nothing at all to say about His coming.

The "proof," in passing, that the Church alone will see the *parousia* (the pre-tribulational return) is the "in a moment" and "twinkling of an eye" language in 1 Corinthians 15:52, which according to pre-tribulationists seems to prove the point, but we are never told how. The other "proof" passage is Acts 1:11 where we are told that only believers saw Jesus go up from the earth at His ascension, *and so* it is ascertained that only believers will see Him return because of the "like manner" language in the text. In fact, it may well be that only Christians saw His ascension, but theology must not be written on the basis of a bias based on an assumption but on clear statements of Scripture. In fact, He left the earth, *terra firma,* and the theorists vehemently contend that He will not actually touch down on the earth at the rapture. If He touches the earth in the rapture, again, all is lost. Thus, the passage should never be used in an attempt to prove or even illustrate a pre-tribulational rapture.

An illustration of Jesus coming "for" His Church, and later "with" is seen by a trip to the airport to pick up my daughter and her children, which looks very different if it is arbitrarily dissected into two trips—my leaving for the airport and my returning from the airport. The description of my leaving in an empty car as I head eastward at sunrise with sunglasses on since it is a fair day appears to be totally different from my returning with a car filled with people and luggage as I drive westward with no sunglasses on and wipers on since it is now a rainy day, and additionally, with a new dent in my fender. Of course, what has been seen is not two trips but two aspects of one trip.

When Jesus comes for us, we will meet Him in the air, and then, immediately, we will turn and descend with Him as He comes down with us, giving us a grandstand view of Armageddon and His devastating victory there. He has come "for" us and "with" us at the same time, precisely as I went "for" my daughter and her family and "with" them on the same trip. Her trip resembles that of Christ (she continues on with it) and mine resembles that of the Church (I meet her and turn back). Such has always been the orthodox teaching regarding the return of Christ.

It has even been suggested by some that were the Church to be taken away from the earth and then to return immediately to earth with the ascending Christ would amount to "God's yo-yoing of His Son's bride." One hesitates to comment. One author, noting the manufactured differences seen by some between the two comings of Christ, has this to say:

This type of argument could be used to prove that there were at least two apostle Pauls-the one who wrote Ephesians and the one who wrote Philippians, for example. The proof could be taken from the salutations alone:

(1) The Paul who wrote Philippians was a bondslave of Jesus Christ, while the Paul who wrote Ephesians was not a bondslave.

(2) The Paul who wrote Ephesians was an apostle, while the Paul who wrote Philippians was not an apostle.

(3) The Paul who wrote Philippians had a close associate named Timothy, while the Paul who wrote Ephesians apparently knows of no such person.[13]

9. Post-tribulationists get Israel and the Church mixed up, spiritualizing the Old Testament promises and granting them not to Israel to whom they were properly given but to the Church.

Such an idea is stated often in many ways by pre-tribulationists. In fact, it is in the minds of many pre-tribulationists the argument *par excellence,* against post-tribulationism. Only dispensational pre-tribulationists in their view get the Israel and Church dichotomy right. H. C. Thiessen, for instance, says that, based on Daniel's seventy weeks, the Church can't be on earth during the final week which is the tribulation period because, throughout the first sixty-nine weeks, God is dealing with Israel and only with Israel during the time of "Jacob's trouble." Then, during the break (or "hiatus" as the theologians call it) between the sixty-ninth and the seventieth week, God is dealing with the Church and only the Church. Then, in the seventieth week, God deals again with Israel and only with Israel. That teaching is not at the heart of dispensationalism; it *is* dispensationalism. Literally, a dozen such passages by other dispensationalists could be quoted which establish this teaching as central to pre-tribulationism.

Put another way, the doctrine of the "distinctiveness" of the Church from Israel produced pre-tribulationism. Many post-tribulationists have observed that fact, but it is freely admitted by pre-tribulationists. Ryrie makes this telling comment about the issue:

> The distinction between Israel and the Church leads to the belief that the Church will be taken from the earth before the beginning of the tribulation... Pre-tribulationism has become a part of dispensational eschatology. Originally this was due to the emphasis of the early writers and teachers on the imminency of the return of the Lord; more lately it has been connected with the dispensational conception of the distinctiveness of the Church.[14]

This is an admission that a hermeneutical necessity produced pre-tribulationism and not the explicit statements of Scripture. Ryrie's admission explains why pre-tribulationists admit that the teaching of a pre-tribulational rapture is not explicit in Scripture and is an inference. Ryrie might have said instead of the Church-Israel distinction *leading* to the belief that the Church will be taken from the earth before the beginning of the tribulation that it *produces* such a teaching. By "hermeneutical necessity," I mean that, although the Scriptures do not explicitly—or even implicitly—teach such a thing, theological preconceptions demand that certain meanings be given a word or a text. Such a process is called "eisegesis," that is, literally, leading into the text what is not there, as contrasted with "exegesis," that is, leading out of the text what is there. (Hermeneutics is the science of interpretation.)

Walvoord goes to great lengths to define the tribulation period in such a way contending that it deals only with Israel and not with the Church so that he can conclude with this shocking statement: "The presence of the true Church [in the tribulational period] is wholly unnecessary."[15]

What about the supposed disconnection between God's two peoples, Israel (His "earthly" people) and the Church (His "heavenly" people)? Are they as disparate as the theorists contend?

Such a theory is totally arbitrary; it is a grid superimposed, gratuitously, upon the Bible and history, and is totally without foundation. Not a scintilla of evidence exists that the Church will not be touched by the events of the seventieth week. In fact, the opposite is true.

At the heart of this entire matter is the view of supreme importance to dispensational pre-tribulationism that God has one plan for Israel and another for the Church, and the two are totally different and must not be confused. The Church and Israel are two wholly differing peoples, and God's plan for each is totally disconnected with the other. This matter is so crucial to pre-tribulationism that Charles Ryrie says: "If the Church is fulfilling Israel's promise as contained in the new covenant or anywhere in the Scriptures, then (dispensational) premillennialism is condemned."[16]

The demonstrable fact, obvious to all students of the New Testament, remains to be that some promises made to Israel have, in fact, come true in the Church. That is not to deny that such promises will one day come true in final fulfillment for Israel. Christians find various ways of dealing with that fact, but the fact itself is undeniable.

Because post-tribulationists hold that some (many would say "all") of the promises made to Israel come true for the Church, pre-tribulationists are wont to say: "Post-tribulationism is based on a denial of the distinction between Israel and the Church." Such an allegation is not true, and to say such is a denial of demonstrable fact and is seen by many as little more than a scare tactic.

Among the most prized books in this author's collection are two unpublished doctoral theses dealing with this precise issue. The first was produced by Daniel P. Fuller in 1957 at Northern Baptist Theological Seminary under the title of "The Hermeneutics of Dispensationalism," and the other (previously cited) was written by William E. Bell, Jr. in 1967 at New York University. Interestingly, Dr. Bell is an honored graduate of Dallas Theological seminary, the educational hot-bed of pre-tribulationism. During his student days there, as happened to so many others, he came to change his view of end-time events from pre-tribulationism to post-tribu-lationism. Fuller and Bell shred the dispensational pre-tribulational hermeneutic, particularly as it relates to the Israel and Church relationship.

To deal with the biblical message regarding the supposed Church and Israel hiatus, it will be helpful to begin with the new covenant promised to Israel in Jeremiah 31:31-34 because the fulfillment of that covenant poses an insoluble problem for the pre-tribulation position. The pre-tribulationist's position cannot admit that the Church operates under the provisions of that covenant because it was made with Israel and not the Church. If the Church participates in that covenant: (a) the Church inherits promises made to Israel, a thing unacceptable to pre-tribulationism, and (b) if the covenant comes true for both Israel and Church, then God is dealing with the Church and Israel at the same time which is totally unacceptable to pre-tribulationism. The distinction between the two groups is total, and they must, at all costs, be kept inviolably separate.

Dwight Pentecost struggles valiantly and at length with the problem in his pre-tribulational classic, *Things to Come*. He, on the one hand, does not want to say that the Church inherits the promises made to Israel. If that were true, he says, the millennium (when Israel will experience the fulfill-ment of many of God's end-time promises) would be unnecessary. A-mil-lennialism does precisely this and, thus, sees no reason for an earthly mil-lennium at all. On the other hand, he has difficulty holding to the position (in the face of so much New Testament material and the admission of the fact by other leading lights in pre-tribulationism) that the provisions of the new covenant do not in any way touch the Church.

In *Things to Come*, he cites three ways of dealing with the problem. The first, he says, is to take Darby's approach. Darby says that the Church "gets the benefit of [Jeremiah's new] covenant" but that the covenant will be "made good to Israel by-and-by."[17] He further quotes Darby as saying, "We enjoy all the essential privileges of the new covenant...but that the covenant 'will be established formally with Israel in the millennium.'"Then, later, he quotes this difficult sentence from Darby: "It is, then, the annexed circumstances of the covenant with which we have to do and not the formal blessings which in terms have taken place of the conditions of the old, though some them may, in a sense, be accomplished in us."[18]

Darby admits that the Church partakes in the provisions that the new covenant made to Israel, which will ultimately be fulfilled in Israel later. To say such a thing is to admit openly—no matter what verbal gymnastics are employed—that a promise made to Israel comes true in and for the Church. His problem, obviously, is that he along with other pre-tribulationists does not want the Church to inherit all the promises made to Israel but was confessedly aware that, somehow, some of the provisions of the new covenant made to Israel had come true in the Church.

Pentecost's second way of dealing with the problem is that of Scofield who, he says, sees "one new covenant with a two-fold application, one to Israel in the future and one to the Church now."[19] The believer, then (according to Lincoln, agreeing with Scofield) "...partakes of the Lord's Supper in remembrance of the blood of the New Covenant...and is also a minister of the New Covenant (and)...He benefits from the New Covenant." Grant (also agreeing with Scofield, et al.) is quoted as saying, "...If we have not the covenant made with us, it can yet, in all the blessings of which it speaks, be ministered to us."[20]

Thus, Pentecost admits that Darby, Scofield, Lincoln, and Grant all know that a promise made to Israel did, in fact, in some sense and to some extent, come true for the Church. Indeed, Grant speaks of "*all* the blessings of which it (the New Covenant) speaks" as coming true for the Church. Pentecost disagrees with these aforementioned leading pre-tribulationists, saying: "This [second] view places the Church under the new covenant, and views the relationship as a partial fulfillment of the [new] covenant."[21]

A third view (and the one Pentecost espouses) of the relationship of the Church to a covenant given to Israel is the "two-covenant" view, believing that one "new" covenant obtains for Israel and a second "new" covenant, although never mentioned in the Old Testament, obtains for the Church, and the two have absolutely nothing to do with each other. Pentecost quotes Walvoord extensively as affirming this view which says that the references to the new covenant in Hebrews do not put the Church under that covenant at all but simply states that it will be when it becomes operative later for Israel, superior to the old covenant given by Moses. The writer of Hebrews does not say that the Church operates under the new covenant, he says. The writer "does not state that what is promised there is now operative or effectual" in the Church or Israel either for that matter. He concludes by saying, "It is a misrepresentation of the thinking of the writer to the Hebrews to affirm that he teaches that Israel's new covenant is now operative with the Church."[22] Which causes one to exclaim, "What, then, could be the writer's reason for mentioning the new covenant at all, or indeed, for even writing the book of Hebrews?"

John F. McGahey, himself a dispensationalist, in his doctoral thesis at Dallas Theological Seminary on the subject of the new covenant, comes to a very different conclusion:

> It has been evident from this study that the theory of the two new covenants was born of controversy rather than sound exegesis. For it appears that it was manufactured to avoid the assumed conclusion that to relate the Church to Israel's new covenant necessitated the Church fulfilling promises given to Israel under that covenant.[23]

Many students of the entire subject would agree, lamentably, with McGahey's observation that much of dispensational theory and not only that in regard to the new covenant was born out of controversy and not out of sound exegesis. All this is of a piece with another observation by Bell: "This facility to provide additional complications (when pushed to explain away what is obvious in the New Testament) is highly developed in pre-tribulational circles."[24]

What do the New Testament Scriptures teach about the Church's relationship to the new covenant? First, Jesus, in instituting the Lord's Supper, plainly said, "For this is the blood of the new testament (or covenant), which is shed for many for the remission of sins" (Matthew 26:28; the Greek is *touto gar estin to aima mou to tes kaines diathekes to peri pollown ekchunomenon eis aphesis amartion*). "*Estin*" translates as "is" not "was" or "will be" or "is" in some limited sense. "*Kaines*" is "new" in contrast to "old." The disciples, as students of what we call the Old Testament, clearly understood what Christ was saying: "This is the new testament, the new covenant promised by Jeremiah (31.31f), which I am now inaugurating, which takes the place of the old testament, or old covenant, which is now superceded by this new covenant."They knew of a new covenant to come, knew of only one new covenant to come, knew that it would replace the old, and knew that it was now being inaugurated. Either that or words mean nothing, and His followers were plainly told that they were at that moment enjoying its provisions, produced by the very blood of Jesus Himself.

Further, Paul teaches the Corinthians precisely the same truth. The event of the Supper established the new covenant for them and their day. In 1 Corinthians 11:25–26, Paul reports what the Lord Himself revealed to him about the institution of the Supper. That is not to say the event exhausted the prophecy. Obviously, it did not in view of the promise that at Jesus' return the new covenant will become operative for Israel (upon their conversion) as we know from Romans chapters nine through eleven.

It is important to discuss another issue at this juncture. It is commonly held that probably all but at least one of Jesus' apostles were Jewish as were many of his disciples. When they came to saving faith in Him, what happened to their Jewish ethnicity? Were they still to be considered as Jews or not? And if so, to what extent? Were they, in being saved, entering into the promise of Jeremiah's new covenant or not? And what special treatment if any could they legitimately look forward to as Jews in the millennium? Did not saved Jews and Gentiles comprise one reality, the Church, which is the body of Christ? If so, what are the implications for the "two separate and distinct bodies, Israel and the Church" which dispensationalists make so much of? In 2 Corinthians 3:6, Christians are told that they are "able ministers of the new testament," a testament which is contrasted in the context with the old testament or covenant. How can that mean anything except that what the disciples had experienced they were now charged with announcing to their world? What were they to say about the new covenant? That one day, in the dim and distant future, it was going to come true for Israelites but had nothing to do with them? That they were purveying a message which was entirely designed for the future and not for their day? Or that, though they had experienced one "new" covenant already, the truly "new" covenant, the Old Testament "new" covenant, would come a day in the future? Not at all. Their message essentially proclaimed, "We have experienced the truth of the new covenant and are now sharing that with Jew and Gentile alike, all the while praising God for making good in our day His promise of a new covenant to come."

An essential point of the Book of Hebrews is that current believers operate under the blessings of the new covenant which has superceded the old, or let it be said plainly; otherwise, the heart is ripped out of the message of the book. In Hebrews 7:22, we read, "By so much was Jesus made [past tense] a surety of a better testament [or covenant]." In Hebrews 8:6, we are told that "he obtained [past tense] a more excellent ministry, by how much also he is [present tense] the mediator of a better covenant which was established upon better promises." ("Was established" is *nenomo thetetai,* a Greek perfect tense verb, denoting an action completed in the past with results in the present.) In Hebrews 10:9–10, we read, "Then he said, 'Behold, I have come to do Your will, O God.' He takes away [present tense] the first that He may establish the second. By that will we have been sanctified [past tense] through the offering of the body of Jesus Christ once for all." The passage states that He takes away the first so as to establish the second. "We have been sanctified" and not "We will one day be sanctified." Not "Some day the Jews will be sanctified, and we are simply announcing that fact to you before it happens," but "We stand sanctified by the provisions of the new covenant which we have experienced and are announcing to everyone." None of that, again, is to deny the coming blessings of the salvific provisions of the new covenant for the Jews in the future; it is to deny the fallacious belief that Christians do not operate under the provisions of the new covenant now.

An excellent illustration of the relationship of the Church and Israel, and an unanswerable one for the pre-tribulationists, is the event of Pentecost where Peter, observing the phenomena of the day and knowing the Jewish Scriptures well, rose and stated under the inspiration of the Holy Spirit, "This is that which was spoken by the prophet Joel..."This is that," not "this is *like* that" (Acts 2:16).

Every student of the English language knows the function of the word *that* in the above statement is that it serves as a predicate nominative; that is, it is synonymous with the subject. In this case, "this" is the subject and "that" is the predicate nominative which "identifies" the subject. The two things—what Joel prophesied and the coming of the Holy Spirit—are, therefore, one and the same thing. What we have here is a prophecy given to the Jews being applied to both Jews and Gentiles. The majority of post-tribulationists are agreed that Joel's prophecy will one day come true for national Israel when Jews are converted to their Messiah Jesus according to Romans eleven. In doing so, it will manifest itself in double fulfillment as is often the case with biblical prophecy.

Walvoord makes a fatal admission on this passage: he tacitly admits that Joel's prophecy, which he admits was made to Israel, came true for the Church, adding, as all biblically-based non-dispensationalists would, that the prophecy will "have its complete fulfillment" in the future.[25] If it is to be "completed" in the future, it must be operative now.

"Fatal?" Yes, for dispensationalists. To allow Joel's prophecy or any other made to Israel as Ryrie and others do to come true in the Church is a patent denial of their Church/Israel hiatus and thus of dispensational pre-tribulationism. The noted apologist Bernard Ramm says:

> The New Covenant is one of the several items discussed in Hebrews all of which are now realized in the Church and the present age. That Christ is our Moses, our Aaron, our Sacrifice the strict literalists readily admit. To isolate the New Covenant and forward it to the millennium is to disrupt the entire structure of Hebrews...To say that we are under the benefits of the covenant without actually being under the covenant is to clandestinely admit what is boldly denied.[26]

In fact, tellingly, many terms used of Israel in the Old Testament are used of Christians in the New Testament. Christians, like Jews, are labeled "the circumcision" (Philippians 3:1–3), "the elect of God (Colossians 3:12), "the diaspora" (James 1:1 and 1 Peter 1:1), "a chosen generation" (1 Peter 2:9), "a royal priesthood" (1 Peter 2:9), "a holy nation" (1 Peter 2:9), "His own special [or "peculiar," KJV] people" (1 Peter 2:9), "the seed of Abraham" (Galatians 3:26–29), possessors of the kingdom (Luke 12:32), and inheritors of the new covenant (2 Corinthians 11:25–26). Further, significantly, Christians have been grafted into the stock of Israel according to Romans 11:17. Why then wouldn't the New Testament writers have been much more careful to stay away from such terms if the hiatus between the Church and Israel was as clean-cut and disparate as the dispensational position contends?

10. How can God deal with both peoples, Israel and the Church, at the same time? This is the Church Age which ends with the rapture. After the rapture, God will begin to deal with the Jews again.

A classic statement of that position is written by Hal Lindsey: "But the Scriptures make a vast distinction between God's dealing with the Church and that time of Tribulation which seems to be a resumption of God's dealing with Israel...During the Tribulation the spotlight is on the Jew-in the book of Revelation the Jew is responsible for evangelizing the world again" (Revelation 7:1–4).[27]

The essential difference between Lindsey's statement and most other pre-tribulationists is the softening word seems; his colleagues are, for the most part, adamant in their belief that such a shift in "dealing" with the two groups will occur.

With whom was God dealing in 70 AD? His Church was reaching out in missionary ministry, and He was judging His people Israel. He was dealing in a substantive and significant way with both Israel and the Church. Whom was God dealing with in 1948? Amazingly, He was allowing the Jews to form a nation after 2500 years of their being dispersed among the nations, and He was dealing with His growing Church all over the earth. And whom is God dealing with today? Obviously, with the nation Israel (whose capital city, Jerusalem, is increasingly becoming the "cup of trembling" to the nations as promised in Zechariah 12:2) and with His Church as she continues her worldwide missionary endeavors.

Plainly, God will deal powerfully with Israel in the future as Paul makes clear in Romans nine through eleven, but two things must be noted. First, the sole blessing promised there is salvation (which is a conditional promise "if they do not continue in unbelief" according to Romans 11:23), and second, that does not prohibit His working with the Gentiles at the same time. Further, no matter when God deals with Israel or how He does so, He will be working with vastly more Gentiles than He does Jews, given the sheer numbers involved.

As to the "Jewishness" of the tribulation period, some basic observations are in order. First, it is, indeed, a "time of Jacob's trouble" (Jeremiah 30:7). It cannot be forgotten, however, that it is a time of troubles for Gentiles as well. It is important to remember that there seems to be a consensus among Jews themselves that approximately fifteen million Jews are living today (remembering the difficulty in defining a "Jew") in a world population of over *six billion*. If that fact is kept in mind, and it is understood that hundreds of millions of people will be slain (and maybe that many saved) during the tribulation period, it is seriously misleading to label it solely or even essentially a "time of Jacob's trouble."

Not only will many more Gentiles suffer and die than Jews, but vastly more of them will also be saved than Jews. If every single Jew living today lives through the entire period (all will not, of course) and is saved, that would be an ingathering of fifteen million Jews, so God be praised! However, it may well be that hundreds of millions of Gentiles (Revelation 7:9 reveals an innumerable multitude from the nations of the earth) will be saved. Is the tribulation "Jewish"? Yes, it is, for it is then that God will deal wondrously with Jewish people, but He will also deal with hundreds of millions more Gentile people.

11. Is not the eschatology of Jesus and Paul hopelessly irreconcilable unless we understand that the Gospels deal with God's plan for the Jews and Paul deals with God's plan for the Gentiles?

Does not coherence demand, for instance, that "elect" in the Gospels must refer solely to the Jews and "elect" in the Epistles must refer solely to Gentiles? Such is the theory. It is with this theory that someone approaching Scripture from a liberal position would find here an excellent tactic to use against all conservative Bible-believing Christians: "See, there is among you so-called Bible-loving conservatives those who openly admit that your two leading lights, Paul and Jesus, are hopelessly at odds with each other. Why should any of it be believed?" Such a criticism is wrongheaded, but for the uninitiated, it could have disastrous effects and can only be the logical consequence of pitting the eschatology of Jesus against that of Paul.

And to those Bible-loving conservatives who might be reading these lines, surely this "irreconcilability" brings to mind statements made by theological liberals: "The Gospels and the Epistles are hopelessly incongruous." "The four Gospels are a maze of irreconcilable mish-mash theologies." "Jesus could have never countenanced much that Paul had to say about marriage." "Jesus never condemned homosexuality and Paul did, making them theological and ethical combatants." The persistent and justifiable message of orthodox theology since Jesus' day is the *unity* of the New Testament, indeed, the entire Bible, not its disunity.

In fact, such a supposed incompatability between Jesus and Paul was never a problem for the early church, but as with the theological liberals, new theories must concoct it, or all is lost for them.

To begin with, how is it, again, that such a dichotomy between the teachings of Paul and Jesus never occurred to anybody in the first eighteen centuries of New Testament study? How is it that not a syllable of such eschatological irreconcilability comes from the church fathers, many of whom were taught by the apostles themselves?

Careful scrutiny has been given to this "irreconcilability" question with one result. It is obvious that Paul got his eschatology straight from the Olivet Discourse.[28] J. Sidlow Baxter says:

> Yet the remarkable feature, which must surely impress all but those who simply will not see, is the singular correspondence between the phraseology here (Matthew 24:30–31), and that which is used in 1 Thessalonians 4:15–18...Then what kind of Bible interpretation is it which can take *exactly the same phrases and symbols* in 1 Thessalonians 5:15–18 and say that *there* they teach a *secret* coming...Nothing can disguise to an honest eye the parallel between Matthew 24:30–31 and 1 Thessalonians 4:15–18.[29]

The use of the word *eklektos* ("elect" or "chosen") in the New Testament occurs about twenty or twenty-one times (depending on 1 Peter 1:1), and apart from how Luke 23:36 references Christ's being *chosen* by God, how 1 Timothy 5:21 mentions "*elect* angels," and how 1 Peter 2:4-6 describes an "*elect*" or "*chosen* cornerstone," every time the word is used in the New Testament, it refers to saved people without any distinction between Gentiles and Jews. To state otherwise is to stand against the entire tradition of the Christian faith, and it is to assign arbitrary meanings to the word based on preconceived theories without the sanction of the text or Christian history.

As previously mentioned, the "Didache" is one of the most important pieces of extra-biblical writing in the Church's possession. In fact, some early Christians thought it worthy of being considered canonical. Its proper title is "The Teaching [*didache* = teaching] of the Twelve Apostles." The "Didache" is an early teaching aid which is divided into four sections. It dates back to 50-100 AD, which means that it was in circulation, and in use, before much of the New Testament was written and while some of the apostles were still alive.

In the Didache, the *eklektos* or the elect in Matthew 24:31 is translated as the English word *church*. Evidently, early Christians knew that the "elect" of Matthew were the same "elect" seen in Paul's epistles, so we again see evidence that the early church knew nothing about differentiating the "elect" in the Olivet Discourse from the "elect" in the Epistles or the Revelation. That is altogether a new doctrine whose provenance is less than two hundred years old.

12. Are we not told to "watch" for Jesus' coming? How could that command mean anything if we must wait for any prophesied events to occur before Jesus raptures His Church?

Paul plainly says in 1 Corinthians 1:8 that we are to wait eagerly for the coming of the Lord. The word is *apokalupsis,* meaning "unveiling," which pre-tribulationists admit refers to Jesus' last return, the one at the end of the tribulation. Plainly, then, we are commissioned to keenly anticipate and look forward to an event that is to occur seven years after the rapture beyond the tribulation.

Perhaps the most quoted passage in the entire Bible by "any-moment" proponents is Matthew 24:42 where we are told: "Watch therefore, for you do not know what hour your Lord is coming," and then verse forty-four, "Therefore you also be ready, for the Son of Man is coming at an hour you do not expect." However, both verses come in a post-tribulational setting. Jesus had just finished His teaching about the nature and extent of the great tribulation, and then He issued His command to watch, meaning, as He Himself said in verse thirty-three, "So you also, when you see all these things, know that it is near—at the doors!" "These things" refers to tribulation events of which He had just spoken. "Watch" (*gregoreo*) is used thirteen times in the New Testament in Second Coming passages, and pre-tribulationists assign only four of those to a pre-tribulationist coming— 1 Thessalonians 5:6, 10 and Revelation 3:2–3, thus denying the necessity of assigning any of the thirteen to such an event.

Furthermore, the teaching of the entire New Testament regarding being watchful means not that Jesus can come at any moment since the New Testament patently denies such a thing but that we should be expectant and passionately serving Him while we wait expectantly for His coming whenever it happens. The exhortations to watch in the Olivet Discourse are clearly in the context of a post-tribulational coming. The same is obviously true of another key "watchful" passage, 2 Peter 3.12, though the word *gregoreo* itself is not used. In fact, in no place in the entire New Testament does an exhortation to watch appear in a passage which demands a pre-tribulational return of Christ.

Jesus told us: "Watch therefore, for you know neither the day nor the hour in which the Son of Man is coming," and if the "abomination of desolation" occurs midway through the seven-year tribulational period, we, in fact, can date the precise time of Jesus' coming. He Himself said that to do so was impossible, or so it is said.

Precision demands that we take Jesus' words about our knowledge of the time of His coming exactly as He spoke and meant them, and His exact words are "day" and "hour," not "week" or "month." We may well know the general time frame, assuming we know the precise moment of the "abomination" and yet still not know the precise moment of His return. All that is in perfect accordance with His illustration of a woman bearing a child. We can know the approximate time of her delivery in advance but neither the day nor the hour.

In any case, when Jesus told us to "watch," He knew that He would not return for almost two thousands of years. We cannot say He has been surprised by that vast interval of years, and yet in the face of that knowledge, He told us to "watch."Which means, patently, that He saw no inconsistency between us watching and His delaying His coming for almost twenty centuries. "Watching" for Him, we now know for certain, could not possibly have demanded an "any-moment" return on His part.

But aren't we in danger of being the evil servant who said in his heart, "My master is delaying his coming"? Jesus' criticism is not that the servant observed the obvious-that his master was delaying His coming, for Jesus Himself promised to delay His coming. His criticism was, rather, that he began "to beat his fellow servants, and to eat and drink with the drunkards"; that activity brought about his judgment (Matthew 24:48–51).

13. If Jesus comes post-tribulationally, who will populate the millennium in mortal bodies?

It is commonly asserted by pre-tribulationists that a seminal reason, indeed, some say the chief reason, why the rapture must occur before the tribulation is that if the rapture/return is a single event, there will be no mortals left to populate the earth since all unbelieving mortals will be slain in the final seven years of human history. Pre-tribulationists almost universally insist that all unbelievers will be slain during the tribulation period, culminating in Armageddon. If so, of course, no unbeliever can enter the millennium in a mortal body.

Consider what is going to happen when Christ returns. Believers (whether living or dead) will be taken away in a millisecond, they will meet Christ in the air, and they will immediately return with Him as He scatters the nations which have gathered against His people in the battle of Armageddon. At some point during that very brief time frame, every eye shall see Him, including millions of unbelieving Jews, many and perhaps even most of whom will be saved when they see Him returning (Zechariah 12:10 and Romans 11:26–27).

Now, what happens to such just-saved Jews? Will they be raptured immediately, or will they be left on earth, saved but in their mortal bodies? Obviously, since the rapture is only for those who are already saved when it occurs, they will miss the rapture and live on earth if they escape the ravages of Armageddon—saved but in their mortal bodies.

All that says nothing about the hundreds of millions, if not billions, of Gentiles who will be left after Armageddon. Even though many nations of the earth will come against Israel at the end, many people, again, perhaps billions, will live through the event. Obviously, "all the nations" coming against Israel cannot mean that every living human being will be present in view of the fact that the nation of Israel cannot hold a hundredth part of the world's population. Further, countless numbers of those remaining could well be saved as they see Christ coming. John tells us: "Behold, He is coming with clouds, and *every* eye will see Him, even they who pierced Him. And all the tribes of the earth will mourn because of Him" (Revelation 1:7). Again, if such were to occur, what happens to these just-saved Gentiles? They will have missed the rapture, of course, so they will enter the millennial period saved and in their mortal bodies.

Zechariah's prophecy is an especially interesting study in this regard. In two of the book's final three chapters, the Gentile nations which come against Jerusalem are referenced eleven times: "all the surrounding peoples" (12:2), "the peoples" (12:4), "the surrounding peoples" (12:6), "all the nations" (12:9, 14:2, 14:16, and 14:19), "nations" (14:3), "all the people" (14:12), "all the surrounding nations" (14:14), and "the families of the earth" (14:17). It is obvious that those gathered against Israel will not be believers. Christians (not to mention practicing Jews) will clearly understand the nature of the battle and refrain from attacking God's people.

What happens to all these admittedly unsaved Gentile nations (or "peoples") which have gathered against Israel? They will be thoroughly defeated, and many will be killed. However, many will not be killed but will live through the ordeal. Many of them will surely believe in Christ as will the Jews when they see Him coming in clouds of great glory. Those who will not believe will be forced to worship the newly-installed King in Jerusalem whose reign will last for a thousand years. If they refuse to go up to Jerusalem, they will be punished (Zechariah 14:14–19; "worship" need not mean they worship as saved people but that they acknowledge the authority of the King). In addition, it is to be remembered that such a scenario does not take into account the innumerable millions who will not be in the region but who will be scattered throughout the nations of the earth.

When faced with the Gog and Magog revolt, pre-tribulationists theorize that the rebels are unconverted children of saved parents, which would explain lost people in mortal bodies living during the millennium. In fact, Bell says that many Old Testament passages indicate that unbelievers will live through Armageddon and populate the millennial period. He cites Isaiah 66:15–20, Isaiah 37:32, 45:20, 60:12, Joel 3:7–8, Micah 4:2–3, 7:17, Zechariah 8:23, and 14:16–17. He says:

> Some of the younger pre-tribulational scholars have begun to recognize this line of teaching (i.e., that all unbelievers will not be slain at or before Armageddon), holding that only the actively-rebellious unbelievers will be destroyed at the second advent, fulfilling passages such as Revelation 19:15–18, Jeremiah 25:31, etc....Furthermore, Matthew 25:31ff. pictures a judgment which pre-tribulationists see as the judgment of living Gentiles immediately following Christ's second advent. It is difficult to see how the unbelievers could still be present for such a judgment if they have been summarily removed from the earth at the Second Coming proper. Therefore, it must be concluded that Matthew 24:40–41 is a further description of the event already described in verse 31, i.e., the supernatural gathering of the elect at the Second Coming of Christ. The context will bear no other interpretation.[30]

14. Pre-tribulationism is the ancient doctrine of the Church, admittedly, with *"certain refinements added."*

The italicized phrase is a favorite among pre-tribulationists. Is it admitted, then, that the early church and the New Testament actually enunciated a post-tribulational position which was later "refined" in the 1830s? Is such a refinement still going on? Is there any way modern exegetes can know when such a "refinement" will end? How can a pre-tribulational teaching be called a mere "refinement" when it is sufficiently substantive to prevent hundreds of millions of Christians from suffering the horrors of the tribulation? Its proper description, if pre-tribulationism be true, is not "refinement" but "revolutionary." If it is but a "refinement," what explains the passion with which it is promulgated throughout the earth as if it, and it alone, is worthy of acceptance as biblical orthodoxy with expositors labeling it one of the "fundamentals of the faith"? How is it that those who believe such a "refinement" think that watching and waiting for it *defines* New Testament eschatology, and how can but a "refinement" be used against those who do not espouse it to deny them pastorates, teaching positions, and missionary service opportunities? How could it be used to disallow students to attend certain schools without signing a statement of belief in the doctrine? Or to be allowed to graduate, though having completed all graduation requirements except to accept the new theory as being true? How could it be used to deny church membership in thousands of churches across America? Alas, how could some say (as did the famed radio preacher M. R. DeHaan) that those who teach otherwise are deluded by Satan?[31] In such a light, can the doctrine really be called a mere refinement?

15. The New Testament speaks of the Second Coming under various words which must surely be distinguished.

Again, we must deal with another of the famed "refinements" of biblical truth which the early church knew nothing about.

As we have seen, three words are commonly used in the New Testament in regard to Christ's Second Coming: *parousia* (coming or presence or arrival), *apokalupsis* (revelation, unveiling), and *epiphaneia* (appearing or out-shining or manifestation). Many other words are used of the event (Matthew twenty-four), but these three manifest distinctions, so the elder pre-tribulationists tell us, cannot be harmonized into one event.

A study of the New Testament indicates that these words are used inter-changeably of the return of Christ. To the author's knowledge, in con-tradistinction with older pre-tribulationists, all modern pre-tribulationists admit that the three terms are used in the New Testament of both aspects of Jesus' return. Such plasticity of word meanings call into question the legitimacy of the pre-tribulational grid superimposed on New Testament materials. However, despite such a history, the theorists do not give up the split return, even though they admit that all three of the words are used of each of the two events.

The theory is that Christians are not to look for signs of the rapture (since it is signless and secret, although many modern pre-tribulationists have given up the secrecy of the event what with the shout, the voice of the archangel, the trump of God), and that multitudinous signs precede the revelation (*apokalupsis*) or appearing (*epiphaneia*) which comes seven years later. Orthodox eschatology has always known, however, that the New Testament does in fact teach that signs are to precede the catching away of the Church (for instance in 2 Thessalonians 2:1–3 where the *parousia* is mentioned specifically with precursive signs of the event). Historic ortho-doxy further stated that we are, indeed, told to look for and to await eagerly the revelation, a word classic pre-tribulationism taught (and some teach today) can only refer to Christ's final coming. In 1 Timothy 6:14, for instance, we are encouraged to live "without spot, blameless until our Lord Jesus Christ's *epiphaneia,* and in 2 Timothy 4:8, Paul looks forward to being crowned with the crown of righteousness along with all who "love His *epiphaneia.*"

We then must ask how we could be told to look for and to eagerly desire an event that is seven years beyond the supposed pre-tribulational rapture which brings only judgment upon unbelievers and not deliverance to the Church when the Christians are not even on earth.

The various designations for the day in no way demand two different events; they are simply, as could well be expected, various ways of describing the unimaginably complex and many-sided single event.

16. But is not the purpose of the tribulation to save Israel and judge a God-hating world? And if so, what is the Church doing there?

Here's how Paul Enns, a pre-tribulational theologian, says it:

> The nature and purpose of the Tribulation is important in resolving the issue of the Church's participation in it. (1) Nature of the Tribulation. It has already been shown that the Tribulation is a time of the outpouring of the wrath of God (1 Thessalonians 1:10; Revelation 6:16, 17; 11:18; 14:19; 15:1; 16:1, 19); it is a time of punishment (Isaiah 24:20–21); a time of trouble (Jeremiah 30:7; Daniel 12:1); a time of great destruction (Joel 1:15; 1 Thessalonians 5:3); a time of desolation (Zephaniah 1:14, 15); a time of judgment (Revelation 14:7; 16:5; 19:2). If the Church is the object of Christ's love, how can it be present during the tribulation?

The same author follows with this as to the purpose of the tribulation: "The first purpose of the Tribulation is to bring about the conversion of Israel, which will be accomplished through God's disciplinary dealing with His people Israel (Jeremiah 30:7; Ezekiel 20:37; Daniel 12:1, Zechariah 13:8–9). The second purpose of the Tribulation is to judge unbelieving people and nations (Isaiah 26:21; Jeremiah 25:32–33; 1 Thessalonians 2:12)."[32]

What has the author done? He has defined the tribulation in strict accordance with the pre-tribulational viewpoint which bears but little resemblance to the complete scriptural view as to the *essential* nature of the period. Yes, of course, the tribulation is a period of the outpouring of the wrath of God, but to begin with, such an outpouring in its final intensity does not characterize the entire period. Very obviously, things worsen during the period, culminating in the final days with some exegetes saying that God's final and ultimate wrath possibly marking only (literal) hours at the end of the seventh year. The progression of the intensity of God's wrath whenever it begins in the period is patently manifest in the progressive intensification of the seal, trumpet, and bowl judgments. What does that intensification mean if not that the trauma of the period deepens with passing time?

Merrill C. Tenney, noted pre-tribulationist, says that the tribulational troubles are not of the same intensity throughout the period but accelerate toward the end. They become "more intensive and extensive." He adds: "The brief descriptions of these last seven (bowl) judgments (vv. 2–12, 17–21) may suggest that they occur in rapid succession..."[33]

It is also to be remembered that even if the full wrath of God marked the entire period, a theory which no post-tribulationist the author is aware of holds, God still is able to deliver His people through it even as He has delivered His people in national and personal crises before.

Note carefully in the first paragraph of Enns quoted above that no mention is made at all of the millions, perhaps hundreds of millions, of tribulational Gentiles who will be converted as described in Revelation 7:9. Why and upon what basis shall that substantive, even defining, aspect of the period be omitted in any discussion of the matter?

To be quite frank, how can anybody acquainted with the Bible ever conclude that, because believers are the objects of God's love, they cannot suffer? That possibility denies the biblical message from beginning to end. What about the millions of Christians who have died for their faith since Jesus' day? Were they not the objects of God's love? And what about the "tribulation saints" who will die perhaps by the millions? Are they blood-bought and beloved of the Father, or are they not?

The idea that as objects of God's love Christians cannot suffer or even die, is, put simply, preposterous. The same thing is to be noted in Enns' second paragraph. Reading it, one would not have a scintilla of evidence of other elemental divine purposes in the period besides saving Israel and judging the nations. Those two things undoubtedly will occur; the Bible is explicit about that. Notwithstanding, much else will occur, including the regeneration of the aforementioned countless millions.

17. The New Testament speaks of several eschatological "days" in reference to Christ's return; those "days," if properly understood, must refer to differing events in differing time frames.

What sort of "days"? A study of the concordances indicates that many "day" references refer to end-time events, the most significant of which in the New Testament for this present study would be:

1. "the day," as in 1 Corinthians 3:13, Hebrews 10:25, and 2 Peter 1:9.

2. "that day," as in 2 Timothy 1:12, 1:18, 4:8, etc. (It is so designated at least a dozen times.)

3. "the day of Christ," as in Philippians 1:10 and 2:16.

4. "the Day of Jesus Christ," as in Philippians 1:6.

5. "the day of God" as in 2 Peter 3:12 and Revelation 16:14.

6. "the day of the Lord," as in 1 Thessalonians 5:2, 2 Thessalonians 2:2 (RV; KJV has "day of Christ," but all admit that the RV is correct), and 2 Peter 3:10.

7. "the day of the Lord Jesus," as in 1 Corinthians 5:5 and 2 Corinthians 1:14.

8. "the day of our Lord Jesus Christ," as in 1 Corinthians 1:8.

9. the "Son of Man's" day, as in Luke 17:24 (see also 17:30).

10. "the great day," as in Jude 6, Revelation 16:14 and 16:17.

12. "the day of judgment (or wrath)," as in Matthew 11:22, 11:24, 12:36, Mark 6:11, Romans 2:5, 2:16, 2 Peter 2:9, 1 John 4:17, Jude 6, and Revelation 6:17.

13. "the last day," as in John 6:39–40, 11:24 and 12:48.

What do such days mean according to the theorists? The day of Christ, it is maintained, refers to Christ's coming at the rapture, and the day of the Lord refers to His final coming. He comes first secretly (many say) and signlessly (all say) for the saints, and He comes latterly in open fashion to take the "tribulation saints" home and judge the nations, or so it is taught.

After maintaining those distinctions vigorously for decades, we are now told by many pre-tribulationists that both comings may be spoken of under any of the "days." If so, how is the doctrine of a split coming of the Lord maintained? The problem is "solved" by arbitrarily defining the "day" spoken of as the rapture or the revelation by, it is said, considering the context. If the "day" referred to in the text speaks of blessing, it refers to the rapture; if it speaks of judgment, it refers to the revelation. When neither subject is spoken of, what is to be done? The reader may attribute it to whichever day he wishes. This is why pre-tribulationists differ among themselves so often about which verse speaks of which "day."

Enns, admitting that the day of the Lord is not totally devoid of blessing, states that 'the day of the Lord' is a term that can be used (1) of any judgment of God in history; (2) of God's judgment in the Tribulation period, (3) of the blessings in the millennial kingdom; (4) of the entire period from the beginning of the Tribulation to the end of the millennium.[34] Thus, he allows both blessings and judgment in the day of the Lord, giving away much ground on the supposed blessing or judgment distinction between the days.

First, it goes without saying that no documentation in the entirety of church history supports such a theory concerning a distinction between the "days" until the dispensational position recently arrived on the scene. Therefore, such a teaching becomes yet another peculiarity of pre-tribulationism.

Second, if the "days" are to be distinguished, Paul issues a death-knell blow to the theory in his statement in 1 Corinthians 1:7–8 in which he uses the various "days" in speaking of the same event: "So that you come short in no gift, eagerly waiting for the revelation [*apokalupsis*] of our Lord Jesus Christ, who will also confirm you to the end, that you may be blameless in the day of our Lord Jesus Christ." Paul labels that day as the day of the Lord, the day of Jesus, and the day of Christ, as well as the *apokalupsis,* the final coming of Christ. He did not separate the days, for the Church has never separated the days and neither should modern exegetes. Paul also says that God will confirm us to the "end," which takes us to the Second Coming of Christ. How could Christians be told to eagerly await a day which they would never see because of having been raptured seven years earlier?

How do theorists get around Paul's obvious position on this matter? They say that actually Paul says here that we should eagerly wait for the *final* Second Coming of Christ, which proves that we can, indeed, though contrary to their teaching, eagerly and joyously look forward to an event beyond the tribulation but that we will have been raptured away seven years earlier immediately before the beginning of the "day" of the Lord, all of which demands that they stretch the "day of the Lord" out to include a previous seven-years-before-the-second-coming rapture.

What do we find in the Scriptures? We find that everywhere all the "days" speak (although sometimes of different aspects) of a unified and single coming of Christ in which both blessing and judgment occur.

In Zechariah fourteen, Christ's feet touch down on the Mount of Olives at His return, thereby blessing and delivering His people and, at the same time, wreaking havoc on the nations of the world gathered for the battle of Armageddon.

In Isaiah 35:4, we read: "Say to those who are fearful hearted, 'Be strong, do not fear! Behold your God will come with vengeance, with the recompense of God; He will come and save you.'" We realize that vengeance and salvation will come on the same day, as Isaiah 40:10 also describes: "Behold, the Lord God shall come with a strong hand, and His arm shall rule for Him; behold, His reward is with him, and His work before Him. He will feed His flock like a shepherd; He will gather the lambs with His arm, and carry them in His bosom, and gently lead those who are with young." Again, we read of judgment and blessing occurring on the same day.

This same truth that the day of God brings both judgment and blessing is clearly and often stated in the other prophets. Joel's third chapter promises the judgment of God in the valley of Jehoshaphat (3:2) where the "Lord also will roar from Zion (verse 16)," but the same chapter promises in the same time frame that "the Lord will be a shelter for His people, and the strength of the children of Israel" (verse 16).

The same truth of severe judgment is predicted in Micah chapter three and blessing in chapter four as a result of the single act of judgment and blessing on Israel. In fact, the message of both judgment and blessing in the day of the Lord is the consistent message throughout Old Testament prophetic literature.

The New Testament outlines future events the same way. The events of 1 Thessalonians 4:13-18 and 1 Thessalonians 5:2 are spoken of plainly as the day of the Lord. His coming to rapture the saved living and resurrect the saved dead is immediately followed by the judgment aspect of the day of the Lord, which means that the day will have brought immense blessings to those who are His and intense judgment upon those who are not His.

Pointedly, believers are told to watch for such a "day of the *Lord*." If the rapture or resurrection will have already taken place, Paul's admonition to watch is meaningless; he could never have said, "Therefore let us not sleep, as others do, but let us watch and be sober," (1 Thessalonians 5:6) if in fact, the rapture/resurrection will have already happened! Again, what an ideal place to inform Christians not to worry because they will have been delivered seven years earlier!

All of that is why, historically, students of prophecy held what the ancient church believed reading how all of the eschatological "days" speak of the same event. G. E. Ladd states it this way:

> The day of Jesus Christ and the day of the Lord are one and the same day, the day of Christian expectation. Christians are to find delight in one another 'in the day of our Lord Jesus' (2 Corinthians 1:14). Here again the object of Christian expectation is the day which is both the day of the Lord and the day of Jesus. Where does the Word of God assert that the day of Christ is to be distinguished from the day of the Lord? Where does it say that the day of Christ occurs before the tribulation while the day of the Lord occurs at its end? These are inferences of good and godly men but not the clear teaching of the Word of God. If any inference is to be drawn, we must infer that the two expressions refer to one and the same day which will bring salvation to the Church but judgment to the world. [35]

Gundry says: "But this distinction (between the various 'days') wouldn't work even if it could be made legitimately. It wouldn't work because whatever the Day of Christ means, Paul told Christians to watch for the Day of the Lord. And the distinction is false in the first place." [36]

Because the question is so central an issue, one must, even if lengthily, quote Alexander Reese on the matter. His language is sometimes caustic, but his keen scholarship is obvious. After carefully exegeting every passage dealing with the various "days" and being thoroughly familiar with the history of the pre-tribulational theory, he comes to this conclusion:

> Having short or convenient memories they [the pre-tribulationists] are insisting in the strongest manner that the *Coming* of Christ synchronizes with the *Day* of Christ. Now, as I have shewn in the first chapter, Darby, Kelly, Mackintosh, and Trotter all taught in the most decided manner that the *Coming* of Christ is one thing, the *Day* of Christ is another; the two are separated by an unknown

period of years. Not only this, when pre-millennial writers like Tregelles, Newton, Muller, Alford, Saphir, West and Erdman taught that the *Day* of Christ was the same thing as the *Coming* of Christ, their teaching was repudiated in energetic fashion by orthodox pre-trib advocates. It was confusing in the extreme, and a betrayal of the blessed hope, to mix it up with the *Day* of Christ; so it was arrogantly asserted.

Now, however, if Gaebelein, Anderson and Scofield are to be believed, the blundering and confusion must be attributed to the past eminent leaders of the pre-trib school of prophecy, for it is now being asserted on the housetops that 'the Day of Christ' synchronizes with the hope of the Church at the Parousia.

It is contended, according to the new school of the new persuasion, that whilst the *Coming* of Christ and the *Day* of Christ are identical, yet they occur long before the Day *of the Lord*. It is this day that concerns Israel and the world, whilst the *Coming* and the *Day* of Christ refer exclusively to the Church. I want the reader to note the remarkable *volte face* ["about face"] in this defense of pre-trib theories; for when properly understood, it reveals in the clearest manner the utter worthlessness of the exegetical foundation upon which the new theories rest. The change occurred as follows: Prior to the appearance of the Revised Version of 2 Thessalonians 2:2, that text read 'the day of Christ' and not 'the day of the Lord' as in the Revised Version. To Darby this change made no difference whatever, for he taught, with commendable consistency, that all these expressions, 'the Day of Christ,' 'the Day of Jesus Christ,' 'the Day of the Lord,' 'the Day of Jehovah,' signified one and the same day. So that even after he had adopted the reading 'Day of the Lord' in his translation of 2 Thessalonians 2:2, he continued to speak of 'the Day of Christ' as synonymous (*Synopsis* on Philippians 2:16). The Revised Version, by eliminating the one unfavorable [his footnote explains 'unfavorable' as against an 'any-moment' coming and

119

rapture, at 'Christ's *Day*,' without previous signs] instance of 'the Day of Christ' at 2 Thessalonians 2:2, proved a veritable godsend, in that it released Philippians 1:6, 9, 10; 2:16; 1 Corinthians 1:7–8, and 2 Corinthians 1:14, for service elsewhere in prophetic charts and programs. But yesterday it was shocking to apply them to the hope: today, shocking to withhold them. In other words, all the favourable texts mentioned above were now coolly and conveniently brought forward by about thirty-five years and applied unabashedly to the blessed hope of the Church! Only the Day *of the Lord* was left at the close of Daniel's apocalyptic Week in order to prop up that part of the new program at the End which continued to assert that whilst the Coming and the Day *of Christ* had no predicted signs or events preceding them, the Day *of the Lord* was to be preceded by signs innumerable, especially by the Apostasy and the revelation of the Antichrist. And those of us who still assert that the Day *of Christ* and the Day *of the Lord* are the same, are looked upon as benighted people, though their identity was a fundamental part of the new system before the R. V. appeared. We can cite page after page from Darby, Kelly, Mackintosh, and Trotter to prove our position.[37]

Three observations can be made regarding the pre-tribulational position on this point. First, it is intriguing that the teaching of J. N. Darby, the historical hero of pre-tribulationism, became taboo to his successors. Second, the very elasticity of the "days" within pre-tribulationalism ought to give pause before differentiating them. Yesterday they meant one thing, today they mean another, and one can only guess what they might mean tomorrow. Third, as is obvious, the perceived unity among pre-tribulationists does not hold up under scrutiny.

18. **But are there not more pre-tribulationists than post-tribulationists?** If the earth did not contain a single post-tribulationist, the teaching would still be correct if that is what the New Testament teaches and incorrect if that is what it does not teach. As to the relative

strength of the two views, Roland Rasmussen, in his *The Post-trib, Pre-wrath Rapture,* quotes several authors to the effect that the majority view of the Church is post-tribulational. He quotes John Walvoord as saying, "Post-tribulationism has long been a common doctrine held by the majority of the Church... *Post-tribulationism,* as far as the Church as a whole is concerned, *is the majority view.*"[38] Rasmussen then precedes to quote several other well-known pre-tribulationists to prove his contention that it is, as it has always been, a minority view.

The Southern Baptist Convention, the largest non-Catholic denomination in America, composed of over 42,000 churches, has adopted, through several successive national conventions, a statement of faith called *The Baptist Faith and Message,* in which a clear-cut post-tribulational return of Christ is affirmed. In the section labeled "X. Last Things," we read the following complete statement on eschatology:

> God, in His own time and in His own way, will bring the world to its appropriate end. According to His promise, Jesus Christ will return personally and visibly in glory to the earth; the dead will be raised; and Christ will judge all men in righteousness. The unrighteous will be consigned to Hell, the place of everlasting punishment. The righteous in their resurrected and glorified bodies will receive their reward and will dwell forever in Heaven with the Lord.[39]

No mention is made of a pre-tribulational return of Christ. Following the post-tribulational statement, a list of Scriptures is given which support the one Second Coming of Christ, including 1 Corinthians 15:35–58, 1 Thessalonians 4:14–18, and 1 Thessalonians 5:1f, the very passages so often quoted by pre-tribulationists in an attempt to prove a pre-tribulational rapture.

No major creed or confession of faith in the entirety of Christendom espouses or has ever espoused a pre-tribulational position.

The Revelation of Jesus Christ

It goes without saying that good people can be pre-tribulationists and that all who love the Lord, His Church and His word—believing what we will about the Second Coming—ought to do all we can to join forces against the devil and his minions. That we ought not to make a doctrine which most Bible-loving people would not hold as necessary to salvation a test of ortho-doxy is also a given, and this author stoutly affirms such a position.

It must be said, however, that truth is important, and as a stone dropped into a quiet millpond sends ripples out to the uttermost shores, error, too, sends its deleterious effects throughout the earth. It vitiates everything it touches. Likewise, doctrine has effect.

The work of God on earth calls for every honest student of His Word to put away pet theories, of whatever stripe and no matter how precious, and accept the truth of the biblical revelation—regardless of what it costs in terms of personal friendships, ministry privileges, relationships to honored institutions, or personal humiliation, and to admit one has been wrong if a careful scrutiny of the Scriptures demonstrates that fact. The Bible either teaches pre-tribulationism, or it teaches post-tribulationism; it cannot teach both. As difficult as it might be, every honest student of Scripture must sit under the truth, must submit to truth, and must give up untruth, however passionately and sincerely held for whatever length of time, and joyously receive and embrace God's liberating truth.

Differently put, the only important consideration in the entire matter is that the biblical text be honestly exegeted. All of the questions about who first taught pre-tribulationism, where the idea originated, what Margaret Macdonald saw and what she did not see, who stole which idea from whom, who covered up what and why and when, which theory is most popular and which is least popular, what personal motives might have caused one person to write one thing and another person to write another, all the *ad hominen* arguments, the setting up and demolishing of straw men, which theory is pleasing to the ear and which is not, and even the question of which eschatological system of doctrine has brought more people to Christ (as if we could truly know), all that and more must be put aside. In the end, none of it matters. What does matter is the sheer honor of God and what He as an expression of His honor has revealed to mankind in the Bible, the book He authored.

Viewing pre-tribulationism from such a biblical perspective (and being thoroughly familiar with its history), Nathaniel West, who has been held in high esteem by prophetic students of every view, wrote:

> [The Pre-Trib Rapture] is built on a postulate, vicious in logic, violent in exegesis, contrary to experience, repudiated in the early church, contradicted by the testimony of eighteen hundred years...and condemned by all standard scholars of every age.[40]

Dave MacPherson quotes R. Stanley Payne as saying that Harry Ironside, the godly pastor and author of a pre-tribulational persuasion, wrote, late in his life, in a personal letter: "I know that the system I teach is full of holes, but I am too old and have written too many books to make any changes."[41]

If Ironside made such a statement and *if* the "holes" he discovered were produced by a study of the Bible, then God be praised for his honesty.

Notwithstanding, what Ironside reportedly could not do, many others have done. The list of those who moved from pre-tribulationism to post-tribulationism is impressive and includes exegetical heavy-weights W. J. Erdman, Robert Cameron, Philip Mauro, Rowland Bingham, G. Campbell Morgan,

Oswald J. Smith, and Harold John Ockenga. That does not take into account the excellent exegetes among the Plymouth Brethren themselves who, from the beginning, never accepted the two-coming theory; men like George Muller, S. P. Tregelles, and B. W. Newton, who, along with the aforementioned, represent a veritable "Who's Who" in prophetic teaching. Most of these men were once enamored with the Irving/Darby theory but came to (or more commonly came back to) a full-blown post-tribulationism. Interestingly, the movement is always (as far as the author knows) from pre-tribulationism to post-tribulationism and never the other way around except for some of the earliest proponents of the doctrine who, of course, never held a pre-tribulationist position. However, it is important to state again that neither name nor position nor ability nor popularity, not even one's sincerity and not even personal love for Christ, counts. What counts is what the Bible teaches.

PART FOUR

Believing in a Post-tribulational Rapture

Why Believe in a Post-tribulational Rapture?

I believe in a post-tribulational rapture because it is the consistent testimony of the early church, believed and taught by the apostles and by those who were discipled by the apostles. There was no such term as "post-tribulationism" until well after 1830 and the advent of the Plymouth Brethren. The idea of Christ's coming following a period of unprecedented tribulation was accepted as non-debatable orthodoxy—even by a-millennialists. Nobody spoke of a "post-tribulational" rapture because it was, by that name, a thing unknown and unnecessary since it was commonly-accepted biblical theology. Again, that does not prove the doctrine to be true, but the rule is that the burden of proof always lies on the innovator. It is beyond credibility, if the doctrine be true, that no Christian taught by the apostles themselves ever heard of a pre-tribulational rapture, that not a single soul for the first eighteen hundred years of Christian history did either, and that God would blind His Church to so critical an event as a "pre-tribulational" rapture for the greatest portion of all Christian history.

In the early days of post-apostolic Christian history, in distinguishing orthodoxy from hetrerodoxy, J. W. C. Wand says that "orthodox teachers" identified three marks of heresy. The first one was that it was novel or, in other words, a new teaching. "Nothing could be regarded as properly belonging to the faith of the Church which could not trace its origin back to the apostles."[1] All orthodox doctrines date to the biblical revelation and have been taught throughout Christian history, but one looks in vain for any reference to pre-tribulationism until the mid-1800s.

I believe in a post-tribulational rapture because of the obvious way in which proponents of the pre-tribulational doctrine are forced to twist and distort the clear meaning of Scripture and church history, especially the teachings of the fathers, in an attempt to force passages, both in the Bible and from other sources, to espouse a pre-tribulation rapture.

Commonly, an arcane and arbitrary "dispensational pre-tribulational Church/Israel dichotomy" grid is forcibly superimposed onto Scripture, extraneous ideas are inserted into passages, distinctions are fabricated where none exist (the "days," "kingdom of God versus kingdom of heaven," etc.), and words have their obvious meanings denied (*apostasia* in 2 Thessalonians 2:3; *eklektos* in the Gospels). Interestingly, we likely wait in vain for modern pre-tribulationists to admit what their heroes commonly did in regard to provable distortions superimposed on the fathers' writings.

I believe it because leading pre-tribulationists admit that the teaching is based not on the exegesis of biblical texts but on the basis of presuppositions from which they operate.

I believe it because it is patently taught in the New Testament. The debate is not whether God can end history one way or the other; God the Almighty can and may do whatever He pleases, in any way He pleases, at any time He pleases, and for any reason He pleases, and all thoughtful men will fall on their faces and give Him eternal praise when He does. The issue, therefore, is not what God can or may do; it is what He has said He will do, and Scriptures clearly attest to His plan and purpose to send Jesus back to earth once and not twice at the end of a terrible worldwide crisis and not before.

As Jesus' disciples watched Him ascend into Heaven following His resurrection, "...Two men stood by them in white apparel and said, 'Men of Galilee, why do you stand gazing up into heaven? This same Jesus, who was taken up from you into heaven, will so come in like manner as you saw Him go into heaven'" (Acts 1:10–11). That coming of Christ and that coming of Christ alone is our blessed hope! We search in vain for a single syllable proving the Irvingite illusion of a "secret and signless" coming seven years earlier. What a strange thing for Dr. Luke to say if "the next thing on God's calendar is a 'secret and signless' pre-tribulational rapture seven years before the Second Coming." And how deceptive of the "two men," if a pre-tribulational rapture be true, not to say so. (Again, the "secret" aspect of the rapture so popular among earlier writers has now, largely, been given up by pre-tribulationists.) Those facts demonstrate that the verse applies to Christ's (final) coming as is held by Scofield, Thiessen (in *Lectures in Systematic Theology,* pp. 347, 355, etc.), Walvoord (in *The Revelation of Jesus Christ,* p. 39), LaHaye, (in *Revelation,* p. 13), and many others.

Pentecost has an interesting view of this verse. He is the only pre-tribulational writer of which I am aware who contends that it refers both to the rapture *and* to Jesus' final return. He explicitly says the passage refers to Jesus' first coming as well as to His final coming.[2]

It is in the latter context that he pens this stunning sentence: "It is true that the events of the seventieth week (of Daniel) will cast an adumbration before the rapture, but the object of the believer's attention is always directed to Christ, never to these portents."[3]

However, that is precisely what the ancient church's post-tribulational view taught. It taught that there will occur "adumbrations" and "portents" (which, translated into the vernacular, simply mean "signs") before Jesus comes to rapture His Church away in His final and only Second Coming. Further, they taught that believers were not encouraged to focus on such signs but on His glorious descent to earth following them. Here Pentecost demolishes the pre-tribulationism's famed "signless" rapture because, obviously, if we can see and define signs of Christ's (final) Second Coming, we can certainly know of the nearness of His (presumed) seven-year-earlier rapture. We then are caught doing what, according to classic pre-tribulationism, we should never do which is looking for signs of the rapture!

In any case, this verse is held by some pre-tribulationists to refer to the pre-tribulational rapture because Jesus is said to come "in like manner" as He went away. That means, they say, that He will be seen only by believers when He comes since such was the case when he left. The theory evaporates, however, when, as we have seen, it is observed that if we hold that all the particulars of His ascent into Heaven must apply to His descent, then, of necessity since His feet were on earth when He ascended His feet must touch the earth at the pre-tribulational rapture, a thought which is passionately denied by pre-tribulationists. This theory cannot allow His feet to touch the earth until they touch down, seven years later, on the Mount of Olives as Zechariah promised in 14:4.

In the entire Book of Revelation, written for the sole purpose of preparing the world for Jesus' Second Coming, only one Second Coming is ever seen. In the one book within the entirety of the New Testament in which we would expect to have information about some supposed "pre-tribulational" coming not a syllable is spoken of such an event. Theorists must then create a rapture with the scantiest of materials, including Revelation 2:25 and 3:10–11, John's call in Revelation 4:1, or from the twenty-four elders situated around the throne in Revelation 4:4 (and elsewhere), to create, *ex nihilo,* a "pre-tribulational" rapture.

Walvoord says, "In no other book of the Bible are end-time events portrayed in more detail than in the Book of Revelation." He then adds:

> Even the great themes of the Millennium and the eternal state, while presented specifically in chapter 20 and chapters 21–22, serve only as an epilogue briefly added to a book that has the primary purpose of presenting end-time events in great detail, climaxing in the Second Coming of Christ.[4]

The question, then, is this: why doesn't the "blessed hope of the Church," the pre-tribulation rapture, qualify as an "end-time event" of any substantive significance? In a book of "great" details about end-time events, is it a detail of such utter insignificance that in a list of other details it is not even mentioned? Is the transcendent truth of the coming of Christ for His Church lost in what could be cogently argued by comparison are end-time trivialities? The Book of Revelation is, after all, addressed to seven local churches in Asia Minor.

In *The Rapture Question,* Walvoord himself speaks of the significance of the rapture: "The question of whether the Church will go through the tribulation is not as trivial and academic a question as some would make it. It is rather an issue with great practical and doctrinal implications."[5] He then goes on to argue its significance from an exegetical viewpoint, from a theological viewpoint, and from a practical viewpoint. However, now we are told that "the next event on God's prophetic program" is not specifically mentioned in the entirety of the Book of Revelation.

In fact, to understand the significance of a pre-tribulational rapture for pre-tribulationists, it is only necessary to say it plainly. It is Christ's only Second Coming for His Church! There will never be another. True, according to that view, He will come later with His Church, but His first (rapture) coming is His one and only coming for His Church—the "hope of all our hopes the sum" of the Church, according to pre-tribulationism.

What, then, is Walvoord's explanation of the fact that the rapture is not explicitly referenced in the Revelation? He cannot say, of course, that John didn't know in view of the fact that John wrote much later than did Paul, the reputed first recipient of the supposed pre-tribulational rapture.

In fact, Walvoord, as do most pre-tribulationists, holds that John fourteen's upper room discourse promises a pre-tribulational rapture, which would mean that John must have surely known of the event earlier than Paul. One cannot have it both ways. Either John did not know of a pre-tribulational rapture, and thus, the upper room discourse cannot refer to it, or Paul was not the first recipient of the doctrine, which is classic pre-tribulational doctrine.

Walvoord says that the absence of any mention of a pre-tribulational rapture in the Book of Revelation is that the rapture is simply not in the "prophetic foreview" of the book.[6] This, he says, is in keeping with the fact that the book as a whole is not occupied primarily with God's program for the Church. Instead, according to him, the primary objective is to portray the events leading up to and climaxing in Christ's Second Coming and the prophetic kingdom and the eternal state which ultimately will follow. He adds that from a practical standpoint, however, the rapture may be viewed as having already occurred in the scheme of God before the events of chapter four and following chapters of Revelation unfold.[7]

The theory bristles with problems which beg for explanation. How is it that it is "mentioned" but is not a "doctrine"? How many "mentions" constitute a "doctrine"? Further, is the rapture an event which "leads up to" the "climax" of the Second Coming of Christ or not? And if so, why would it not be mentioned? Then, how is it possible that elsewhere (some would say everywhere) Walvoord espouses the great significance of the rapture and yet says that in the prime prophetic literature of the entire New Testament nothing is said of it except vague references in Revelation 2:25 and 3:11, in which passages nothing at all is actually said about a pre-tribulational rapture unless one comes to them with a pronounced preconceptual bias toward such a view. If they do refer to the rapture, what an anti-climactic event the hope of the Church is envisioned to be! And then, in enigmatic language, we are asked to understand and accept as fact that "from a practical standpoint" the rapture has already occurred. "Practical," one asks, in comparison to what? It is precisely on this point that Bell comments:

> This [the absence of a pre-tribulational rapture in the Book of Revelation] would appear to be a strange phenomenon indeed. Here, in the consummating book of the New Testament, directed specifically to seven historical local churches facing severe persecution and needing desperately some hopeful words from the apostle, John instead directs only three chapters to them and spends the remainder of his time compiling a lengthy eschatological handbook concerning events which were to take place on the earth after the Church is removed and relevant only to a coming Jewish remnant. In the great eschatological book in the New Testament, addressed to the Church, John does not speak [according to the theorists] of

the "blessed hope" of the Church but of the Second Coming, which is the hope [in their view] of the Jewish remnant in the tribulation.[8]

In truth, John deals throughout the book with the next and only future coming of Christ, His final descent to earth to deliver His people and destroy their enemies. John begins his book with a report of that one coming in Revelation 1:7: "Behold, He is coming with clouds, and every eye will see Him, and they also who pierced Him. And all the tribes of the earth will mourn because of Him." That coming, virtually all scholars agree, is His "final" Second Coming. John then ends his book with the report of the same Second Coming in Revelation 19:11f where Heaven opens and King Jesus, "The Word of God," descends from Heaven in a robe dipped in blood.

Every "coming" of Christ between those two passages is the single Second Coming at the end of the terrible time of tribulation to raise or resurrect His people, judge the nations, and enter into His millennial splendor.

If it is supposed (as it is by a few pre-tribulationists) that Revelation 1:7 refers to a pre-tribulational rapture and that "tribes" (*phulai*) is used only of Jewish tribes, then it must be concluded that only Jews will see Him at His Revelation 1:7 return. John, however, uses the same word, here and elsewhere, to speak of all peoples (Revelation 5:9, 7:9, 11:9, 13:9, and 14:6). Notwithstanding, apart from any reference to "tribes," *every* eye, both of believers and unbelievers, we are assured, will see Him.

In the Olivet Discourse, one would never discover any "pre-tribulational" rapture without coming to the passages having an a *priori* or pre-accepted conclusion. We are asked to assume that, before the occurrence of the tribulational events Jesus spoke of Christians who will have been raptured away from the earth, though such is never mentioned. Then, we are also told that the Olivet Discourse is "Jewish ground," instructing the listeners of the essentially *Jewish* horrors of the 70 AD events and of the end-time tribulation period. It has absolutely nothing to do, we are told by many pre-tribulationists, with Christians.

However, if we come to the text and read it, just as it is written, all is clear. Two catastrophes will happen, one in 70 AD and the other at the end of history, and our Lord said what He did here to prepare His people for both events. All students of prophecy are well acquainted with the biblical phenomenon of close-at-hand and far-away prophecies sometimes being blended.

Many Christians, in fact, have come to a proper biblical eschatology by simply taking up Matthew twenty-four, Mark thirteen, or Luke twenty-one and reading the material straight through apart from any extraneous theories being superimposed on the text. "'Immediately *after* the tribulation of those days,'" Jesus says, "'the sun will be darkened, and the moon will not give its light; the stars will fall from heaven, and the powers of the heaven will be shaken. Then the sign of the Son of Man will appear in heaven, and then all the tribes of the earth will mourn, and they will see the Son of Man coming on the clouds of heaven with power and great glory'" (Matthew 24:29–30). It is all as clear as day.

Further, it is also patently obvious that Jesus spoke in that discourse to His own disciples and not to the Jews of the tribulational period as the theorists contend. In doing so, He answered their two-fold question: "Tell us, when will these things [no stone left upon a stone in Jerusalem] be? And what will be the sign of Your coming, and of the end of the age?" (Matthew 24:3). His two-part answer warned them, again, of the fall of Jerusalem in 70 AD and the latter-day tribulation of which the Jerusalem experience would be a foretaste of a tribulation "such as has not been since the beginning of the world until this time, no, nor ever will be" (Matthew 24:21). This warning, by the way, is a firm basis for rejecting any theory as to the possibility of the tribulation having already passed because, heretofore, history has experienced nothing reaching its severity.

If the Olivet discourse is all "Jewish ground" and, indeed, along with the remainder of the Book of Matthew has nothing to do with the Church, then why does Jesus instruct these same disciples in this book how His Church is going to withstand the very gates of Hell (16:18)? Why does He, in this book, teach His Church how to solve problems which arise among church members (18:15f), and why does He on the last Thursday of His life institute the ordinance of the Lord's Supper *for His Church,* as is recorded in this book (Matthew 26:26–29)? Is the supper "Church ground" or "Jewish ground"?

In addition, shall the Church, after 1800 years of worldwide evangelism in obedience to Jesus' "Great Commission" in Matthew 28:19–20, cease and desist from so using His command all the while apologizing to the tribulational Jews for co-opting a command meant for them and not for Christians?

And, finally, if the theorists are right, how is it that our Lord gives the "Olivet Discourse" to His disciples, which we are told represent the Jewish remnant in the tribulation, on Tuesday afternoon of the last week of His life and then tells these very same disciples, who now represent Christians awaiting the pre-tribulational rapture, on the following Thursday evening that He is going away to prepare a place for them and will return one day to receive them unto Himself, so they can forever be in the Father's house with Him in glory? How can it be said that they represent Jews in the tribulation on Tuesday and the Church on Thursday? At precisely what point do their representational responsibilities change?

Walvoord has this to say as to why Jesus did not speak of the rapture explicitly in the Olivet Discourse:

> In His discourse, Christ did not reveal a pre-tribulational Rapture, and post-tribulationists raise the question why this important subject was omitted. The answer, of course, is that up to this time the Rapture had not even been revealed and the subject matter did not concern itself with the Rapture…At this point in their spiritual education the disciples would not have understood the subject of the Rapture any more than they understood the subject of the death and resurrection of Christ.[9]

One responds by observing that the fact that the Rapture "had not been revealed" has nothing to do with the issue; Jesus had a perfect opportunity to reveal it whenever and wherever He wished, and such a critical aspect of His return would have fit perfectly here by preventing huge debates among His future followers for centuries. Further, the subject matter of Christ's discourse surely did concern itself with the rapture of believers; the subject matter is obviously end-time events, and by any definition, the rapture is admittedly a substantive, indeed, central, aspect of those events and is called "the blessed hope" by pre-tribulationists. Although the disciples did not fully understand His death and resurrection, that fact did not prevent Him from speaking of it with these very disciples often, or else how could they ever have come to understand it if He had not done so? How is it, one asks, that the limited "spiritual education" of the disciples was not of sufficient acuity to enable them to assimilate this truth on Tuesday, and yet two days later on Thursday, they were clearly able to understand it? What is it, precisely, that happened in the meantime, in a matter of hours, which enabled them to achieve sufficient theological competence to grasp the truth of a pre-tribulational rapture? It was on the latter occasion, again, when the "let not your heart be troubled" message of John fourteen occurred, which pre-tribulationists hold as a passage that definitely and decidedly promises the pre-tribulational rapture.

Some modern pre-tribulationists have moved away from the older position which found no "Church truth" at all in Matthew, having gone so far in the earlier days of the movement as to say, among other things, that modern Christians should never repeat the Lord's prayer since it properly belongs to millennial Jews and is on law and not grace ground, a view still held by some pre-tribulationists. It is now admitted by most that there is much in Matthew which may be a blessing to Christians in the "Church Age" if interpreted according to proper dispensational canons. It is still commonly contended by most pre-tribulationists, however, that the Olivet Discourse is "Jewish ground."

The troubled believer is promised deliverance from his difficulties when God will "repay with tribulation those who trouble you, and [will] give you who are troubled rest with us when the Lord Jesus is revealed from heaven with His mighty angels, in flaming fire taking vengeance on those who do not know God, and on those who do not obey the gospel of our Lord Jesus Christ" (2 Thessalonians 1:7–8)—that is, at the final coming of the Lord at the end of the tribulation. No amount of linguistic contortions can deny the obvious. Evil men receive judgment, and Christians receive deliverance at the same moment which is the moment of Christ's coming in glory.

One writer, grasping for an explanation, informs us that the emphasis in this verse is not on rest for the believer but upon trouble for evil men.[10] Honest exegetes must deal with what the apostle wrote and admit what he explicitly and clearly communicated instead of superimposing theories on the text. When Jesus returns in glory, it is bad for evil men and good for believers, all at the same moment.

In 1 Timothy 6:14, we are encouraged to "keep this commandment without spot, blameless until our Lord Jesus Christ's appearing [*epiphaneia*]." How can we keep His commandment until His final epiphany if we've been raptured seven years earlier?

In 1 Corinthians 1:7-8, we are plainly told that we should come short in no gift, "eagerly waiting for the revelation [note the word *apokalupsis* which most pre-tribulationists understand referring to the last coming of Christ] of our Lord Jesus Christ, who will also confirm you to the end, that you may be blameless in the day of our Lord Jesus Christ." We are told, clearly, to be waiting for the day of the *Lord,* according to the theorists, a thing the Church is never told to do since she will have been raptured seven years earlier.

Peter never hints, in all his writings, of a pre-tribulational rapture, but rather, he informs us that we should be "looking for and hastening the coming of the day of God" upon which the heavens and the earth will be dissolved (2 Peter 3:12). The theorists would have it that we could never be told to look eagerly for the "day of God" because it is a day of judgment which occurs at Jesus' final coming seven years after all Christians are removed from the earth. How could the Church legitimately be told to look for an event which will occur when Christians have been in Heaven for seven years? This passage quiets the theorists and says what they cannot say: Christians will be on earth until tribulational events beset it.

In Hebrews 9:28, we are told to "eagerly wait for Him [when] He will appear a second time, apart from sin, for salvation." Which "second" coming is that—the rapture or the revelation?

In Revelation twenty, a resurrection is mentioned which is labeled the "first" ressurection. It is not the "second" first resurrection. It is not the latterly first resurrection. It is not the final segment of a divided first resurrection. It is the one and only first resurrection, and it obviously follows and does not precede the great tribulation.

Yes, but we are told, only the martyrs of the "Jewish-oriented" tribulation are resurrected here. The martyrs and their resurrection are indeed emphasized here. The entire Book of Revelation has as one of its major themes the encouragement of those who are called upon to suffer and even die for the cause of Christ during those horrendous days. Nevertheless, again, it must be remembered that in Revelation 9:7, an innumerable multitude will be resurrected at the end of the tribulation. If not then, when? And that does not take into account other tribulation saints, perhaps millions of them, who are not killed in the tribulation but raptured at its end.

It is important to note that, as late as the fall of Babylon in Revelation 18:4, believers are still being told to "Come out of her, my people, lest you share in her sins, and lest you receive of her plagues," obviously indicating that some believers will live through the tribulation. It is to be remembered on that score that Daniel and his friends lived through a time when an image was set up in Babylon for which universal worship was demanded on pain of the loss of life itself, but obviously, all who disobeyed the edict were not slain.

And what of the Old Testament saints? In fact, all believers of both Old Testament and New Testament dispensations are resurrected in Revelation twenty's first resurrection according to what has always been the orthodox faith of the Church.

Even in the Old Testament, we are promised a single return of Christ and only a single return of Christ. Psalm 110:1 says, "The LORD said to my Lord, 'Sit at My right hand 'till I make Your enemies Your footstool.'" On one occasion, the Son will arise from God's right hand, and on one occasion, He will return to the earth, and that one occasion is His post-tribulational return. At the supposed pre-tribulational rapture, Jesus' enemies are notoriously not defeated. In fact, Antichrist will demand worldwide worship for at least the final portion of the yet-future tribulational period. If the psalmist was wrong about the matter, why do we not have any correction to his theology in the New Testament?

Pre-tribulationists make much of the fact that the rapture is nowhere seen in the post-tribulational coming of Jesus. Their oft-stated position is as follows: "If post-tribulationists could just show a single passage where the rapture occurs at the post-tribulational coming of Christ, their position would be established." It is important to understand clearly what the pre-tribulationists are asking.

First, Paul tells us in 1 Thessalonians 4:16–17 that dead believers will be resurrected, which was already a well-known fact among the Thessalonians. He further states that the living believers will be raptured, meaning "caught up" (from the Greek *harpadzo,* "to seize, to carry off by force,"—*while living*—into the presence of the Lord. That answers a question which they apparently did not have the answer to before: "What will happen to living believers when Jesus comes back?" The answer is that they will be "raptured" away from the earth while living.

Second, Paul writes in 1 Corinthians 15:52 that "the dead [believers] will be raised incorruptible, and we [living believers] shall be changed [from the Greek *alasso,* which simply means "to change"]." Again, he says then that dead believers will be resurrected and that living believers will be "changed." He does not specifically state that they will be "raptured," but of course, we may assume the fact. Rigor, however, demands that we state the following: Paul does not specifically say so in this passage. Had we not been given the earlier information in the Thessalonian correspondence, for all we know, living believers might not experience change until Jesus comes down to the earth. The "mystery" here, by the way, is not that of a pre-tribulational rapture, which is never mentioned, but is that living believers will be "changed." It is not the timing of the event that is emphasized but the event itself—the "change."

Third, if one singles out the "catching up" of living believers, it is then critically important to note that such a specific aspect of Jesus' return is mentioned in 1 Thessalonians 4:17 and is never mentioned anywhere else in the New Testament, not even in the passages which pre-tribulationists claim as teaching pre-tribulationism. That is a pivotal fact and critical to any study of the issue. The specific act of such a "rapture" aspect of the Second Coming is nowhere else mentioned, and in the sole place where it is mentioned, nothing is said about it occurring seven years before Jesus' final return to the earth.

Fourth, Walvoord himself, as with those of all schools, says that we cannot expect that every detail of the Second Coming prophecy should be mentioned in every passage dealing with the general subject. "It is not unusual in presenting prophetic events for only selected events to be included."[11] Every knowledgeable student would readily agree with that sentiment. To demand, then, that the "rapture" aspect of the Second Coming be mentioned specifically and separately in the other Second Coming passages or in any other single one of the Second Coming passages is demanding more than we have any right to expect.

Next, the remarkable fact is not that the rapture is mentioned but that is mentioned only once in the hundreds of other New Testament references to the Second Coming. Again, the early church always saw only a single coming of Jesus at the end of history and held that in every passage dealing with that coming the "rapture" aspect is to be accepted on the basis of Paul's explanation to the Thessalonians.

Also, it is to be remembered that the only books in the New Testament written before Paul's teaching of a rapture in 1 Thessalonians (written in 51 AD) were probably Matthew and James, both likely having been written in or about 50 AD. It is not as if the later writers of the remaining twenty-four books of the New Testament, written by Mark, Luke, John, Peter, James, Jude, the writer to the Hebrews (if the author was not Paul), and Paul himself, did not know about the "rapture" aspect of the Second Coming. Apparently, they simply saw no reason to constantly reiterate it.

Last, it is to be carefully noted, too, that the "rapture" in 1 Thessalonians 4:17 is not there or anywhere else as it is said to be pre-tribulational. It is never asserted, not intimated, nor hinted at there or in any other biblical passage that there exists a seven-year gap between the "rapture" aspect of the Second Coming and the coming itself. In fact, such an event is not even inferred as is often stated; it is an idea arbitrarily superimposed upon the Scriptures without a shred of evidence. The idea, as we have noted, was born out of a necessity to get the Church off of the earth before the tribulational period began because that period is designed, we are assured, for the Jews and not the Church. However, nowhere, again, in all of Scripture is such a thing taught. It is a pure conjecture based on dispensational definitions of the tribulational period itself and not on the explicit teaching of Scripture.

We discussed earlier how Ryrie makes a definitive admission in that regard in a passage explaining the basis of the necessity of the pre-tribulational rapture of the Church. Ryrie's admission bears repeating due to the powerful implications emanating from it. Every student of the subject should carefully ponder this passage by a leading pre-tribulationist:

> The distinction between Israel and the Church leads to the belief
> that the Church will be taken from the earth before the beginning

of the tribulation... Pre-tribulationalism has become a part of dispensational eschatology. Originally this was due to the emphasis of the early writers and teachers on the imminency of the return of the Lord; more lately it has been connected with the dispensational conception of the distinctiveness of the Church.[12]

Here we have an astonishingly clear-cut and honest admission from a leader of the movement that a pre-tribulational rapture does not arise from the exegesis of the Greek New Testament but is a theological necessity based upon the "distinctiveness of the Church" in accordance with the dispensational definition of the Church, a definition that was not applied to Scripture for over 1800 years of church history. Further, that dispensational definition of the Church has produced out of necessity forced and novel interpretations of other facets of end-time events.

In fact, the proof that pre-millennialism decidedly does *not* depend upon a dispensational definition of the Church is that for over 1800 years it never heard of such a definition. Pre-millennialism is the faith of the ancient church; dispensational pre-tribulational pre-millennialism is of very recent provenance, having been born not more than about 170 years ago.

Again, then, we are told that unless the study of eschatology begins by accepting dispensationalism's unique and presuppositional interpretation of the Church, the entire enterprise is in vain. This theory, among other things, says that the Church never understood herself until Edward Irving and John Nelson Darby came along in the 1830's, which represents an amazing confession. Bell, in the conclusion of his doctoral dissertation, surmises:

> It must be concluded that the doctrine of the pre-tribulational rapture has arisen from the unfounded and inadequate presuppositions of dispensationalism rather than from an inductive study of the New Testament, and that to perpetuate itself has necessitated a host of strained, highly speculative, and often mutually-contradictory interpretations of otherwise clear New Testament passages.[13]

A final statement for serious perusal by all honest exegetes of the New Testament on the subject comes from "the most learned of American students of unfulfilled prophecy, a scholar who made a lifelong study of the whole field, and wrote two brilliant works of Eschatology," Nathaniel West, who said of the teaching of a pre-tribulational rapture of the Church in response to a tract written Frank White entitled "The Saints' Rest":

> No delusion more pleasing and sweet on the one hand, or more wild, groundless, and injurious to truth and faith, on the other, has ever captivated the minds of men, than this one of an any-moment, unseen, secret advent, resurrection, and rapture, a delusion condemned and exposed on almost every page of the Word of God. An unconditional, immediate, impending, any-moment immenency of an event, detached from all the signs that herald its approach, and which has lasted 1800 years, is an immenency that may last for 1800 years more. Such is not the believer's hope! To watch ourselves, to watch against the snares, subterfuges, sins and temptations that beset us, to watch lest our garments be taken from us, to watch for the improvement of our talents, to watch that our vessels have oil in them—and all in view of an account when the Lord comes, to watch the signs of the times, the events which are the footsteps of the coming Lord, the spread of the gospel, the rise of lawlessness, the increase of apostasy, the interest of Israel, the attitude of the nations, our souls ever directed to the realization of His blessed hope, is to watch for the coming of the Lord, and to wait for His appearing...The question is no longer a question of exegesis with such clear light before us. It is simply a question of ethics with every believer. Have we the right moral disposition toward the truth, or will we still cling to error because we have unfortunately defended it too long; shall we act against the Truth of for the Truth? 'Unto the upright there ariseth light in darkness.'[14]

PART FIVE

**Preparing
to Suffer
for Christ**

How Shall We Prepare for the Coming Tribulation?

If, in fact, modern Christians do take the New Testament scenario seriously, realizing the possibility that, in our own generation, we could be called upon to live in and through the terrible time that is coming upon the earth, how shall we prepare to face such times?

1. Consider the possibility of being on earth during the tribulation. Read Billy Graham's *Till Armageddon,* in which he admits the possibility of Christians now living being on earth during the tribulation and discusses how to prepare for the great future Armageddon, which will mark the climax of world suffering and the ultimate overthrow of evil.[1] As someone who has lived on the Florida coast for years might say: "Prepare for the wind—before the wind blows!"

2. Realize that fellow Christians throughout history believed they would go through the period. They looked with genuine joy and excitement for the time following the great tribulation when their Lord Jesus would return to deliver them and destroy all the rebels in the fall of the great and worldwide Babylonish God-hating society. If they lived in joy with that knowledge, so can we.

3. Stand on the knowledge that God will come through for His people. The entire message of the Bible, from one perspective, is heard in this line of modern hymnody: "God will make a way when there seems to be no way."[2] A London pastor once prayed for "London grace." When a friend inquired as to the meaning of the phrase, the brother said,

"That's grace sufficient to live victoriously for Christ in London." Put the name of your town in the "London" slot and pray that prayer passionately. The most difficult place for you to serve Jesus in all the earth is precisely where you're serving Him. Remember: dying grace is never given until dying grace is needed.

4. Practice dying a little bit every day. Paul once said to his Corinthian friends, "I die daily" (1 Corinthians 15:31). Although we don't know all of the implications of the apostle's statement, we do know that the person who has practiced the art of dying before the dying hour will die well. Practice it then. Practice telling your flesh you're dead to its desires. And act that way. Practice denial. Practice going the extra mile. Practice "suffering for righteousness sake," which in truth means "practice dying daily." Jesus calls us to love as sufficiently to die for another even as He died for His bride (Ephesians 5:25). What evidence is there of that love in your life, not a love coming from legalistic motive but a love springing from joy, precisely as Jesus gave Himself for His dear bride?

    Remind yourself that you cannot live forever. That one day the funeral will be yours. That this life is temporary and not permanent. That your tent will fold one day. That your ship will sail soon to the distant shore. By doing so, you will learn to hold loosely onto this world and all that is in it. As it has been said, "A man who has not been able to give meaning to his own life cycle and accept it in its terminal reality cannot die as a man."[3] Such a person is not truly prepared to live. Christians in the West can learn much about all this from our suffering and dying brothers and sisters around the globe.

5. Count Jesus and His cause as worth suffering for. The first-century believers did. Acts 5:42 states, "So they departed from the presence of the council, rejoicing that they were counted worthy to suffer shame for His name," and many times they endured even more than "shame." They endured beating and in many cases death.

After all, there are some things worth dying for. Why do men and women go off to war except that they know that? And why do men and women go off to a career which demands their best, body, soul, and spirit except that they know that? Why do young men and women stay at home and care for aging or ill loved ones, denying themselves a "normal" life with mates, children, homes and careers except they know? The kingdom of God is, by all odds, that alone which is worth, in a cosmic sense, our all. Before his death in 1945 at the hands of Hitler, German theologian Dietrich Bonhoeffer (1906–1945), contended, "When Jesus calls a person, he bids him come and die." [4] In the call of a believer to die for Christ, one's life is truly saved.

6. Tell everybody you can about Jesus. As soon as you can. In every way you can. It all comes down to that. Jesus told us to "occupy" until He comes again (Luke 19:13). The word is interesting. It is *pragmateusasthe* from which we get our word "pragmatic." It really means to practice, to be busy with, to carry on, or to get on with the business of the coming King. Further, the word is in the imperative mood, the language of command. This is no time to take in sail. No time to debate. No time to be frightened of the times. "He who observes the wind will not sow, and he who regards the clouds will not reap" (Ecclesiastes 11:4). It is a time to act and to act proactively. Let every agent of the kingdom and every agency of the kingdom be at his or her best for Him, knowing that history is moving (rapidly as some signs indicate) toward His return.

7. Live with the terrible events of the end in mind but live above and beyond the events. Every thoughtful human knows that he will have a long life if he is fortunate. He will grow old and will suffer all the shocks to which mortal flesh is heir. And then, he will die. The final statistics are impressive: ten out of ten humans die. Those facts, however, do not prevent us from leading happy, joyous, and productive lives. Man's misery, it has been argued, is not based on the fact that he is going to die but that he knows he is going to die. The Christian coun-

ters that man's knowledge of his own impending death is precisely what makes his life so rich because it teaches him to "count [his] days and so apply [his] heart to wisdom" (Psalm 90:12). The important thing, then, is for us to keep our focus on our Lord Jesus and His kingdom and the high privilege of being His servant.

8. Get anchored in the one kingdom which cannot be shaken when all the other kingdoms of this world will be shaken (Hebrews 12:25–29).

9. Read the accounts of Christian martyrs, beginning with the first, "Deacon Stephen," in Acts 7:51f. Listen to the conclusion of his moving and powerful sermon, and watch the angry mob rage against him and send him to the standing Savior in Heaven. Then, read the time-honored aforementioned classic *Foxe's Book of Martyrs.* (Its subtitle is *A History of the Lives, Sufferings, and Triumphant Deaths of the Early Christian and the Protestant Martyrs.*) It will be read by believers and be a blessing to them until the Lord returns. Read also William Estep's The Anabaptist Story, a riveting account of the sufferings and deaths of many of "the radical Reformation." Take the time to peruse the more recent books on the martyrdom of Christians such as Paul Marshall's *Their Blood Cries Out,* Nina Shea's *In The Lion's Den,* and James and Marti Hefley's *Christian Martyrs of the Twentieth Century.*

In his book, *The Next Christendom,* Philip Jenkins observes the marked distinction between the historic churches of Europe and America and those of the "third world" of Africa, Asia, and Latin America. One of those clear-cut distinctions is the incidence of persecution in the latter and its absence in the former. "Southern" Christendom (his word for "third world" church-life) is experiencing explosive growth and vitality but is doing so in the face of horrific persecution:

> For the average Western audience, New Testament passages about standing firm in the face of pagan persecution have little immediate relevance...Some fundamentalists imagine that the persecutions described might have some future reality, perhaps during the

End Times. But for millions of (third-world) Christians, there is no such need to dig for arcane meanings. Millions of Christians around the world do in fact live in constant danger of persecution or forced conversion, from either governments or local vigilantes. For modern Christians in Nigeria, Egypt, the Sudan, or Indonesia, it is quite conceivable that they might someday find themselves before a tribunal that would demand that they renounce their faith *upon pain of death.*

In all these varied situations, ordinary believers are forced to understand why they are facing these sufferings, and repeatedly they do so in the familiar language of the Bible and of the earliest Christianity. To quote one Christian in Maluku, recent massacres and expulsions in that region are 'according to God's plan. Christians are under purification from the Lord.' The church in Sudan, the victim of perhaps the most savage religious repression anywhere in the world, has integrated its sufferings into its liturgy and daily practice, and has produced some moving literature in the process ('Death has come to reveal the faith / It has begun with us and it will end with us.')...In Guatemala or Rwanda, as in the Sudan, martrydom is not merely a subject for historical research, it is a real prospect. As we move into the new century, the situation is likely to get worse rather than better.[5]

Even as you prepare for such possibilities in your own land, pray for your suffering and dying brothers and sisters in Christ around the globe in obedience to the apostolic command: "Remember the prisoners as if chained with them..." (Hebrews 13:3). Maranatha!

Glossary

A-millennialism: The view that teaches that no actual earthly millennium is envisioned. A spiritualized millennium, however, might occur, either in Heaven or on earth. A-millennialists typically teach that Jesus will return to earth personally but will not inaugurate a thousand-year reign on earth.

Antichrist: A man, the epitome of evil, and the final world ruler who will lead in the persecution of God's people at the end of history.

Day of the Lord: The term may refer to (a) any judgment of God, (b) to God's judgment at the end of history, or (c) to the entire period from the rapture through the millennium. It is not only as a time of judgment but also of blessing.

Dispensationalism: The word means a "stewardship" of God and was historically thought to describe the two basic time-frames of God's dealing with humanity—the Old Testament period and the New Testament period. "Modern dispensationalism," however, is characterized by a grid of usually seven time-frames superimposed on history. During such periods, God deals in different ways with His people, who are judged on different bases during the different ages. It is always associated with pre-tribulationalism.

Hermeneutics: The word is defined as science of interpretation. Related to eschatology, the essential interpretive views are: (a) preterist, i.e., that the prophecies of the Book of Revelation were fulfilled in the early years of Christianity in and around the period of the Roman conquest of Israel, (b) historicist, i.e., that such prophecies have been fulfilled through the long sweep of Church history, (c) idealist, i.e., that the symbols of such prophecies speak of the cosmic conflict between God's people and the powers of darkness, and (d) futurist, i.e., that the prophecies while speaking of events of the early Christian era also foreshadow end-time events. (The two leading futurist schools are *historic pre-millennialism*—meaning that form of pre-millennialism which dates back to apostolic days and *dispensational pre-millennialism* which dates to the 1830s.)

Imminence: A word used by pre-tribulationalists to refer to the timing of Christ's return, i.e., that, following His ascension, Christ could have returned at any moment without any prophesied event having to occur beforehand. It does not teach that *today* no prophesied event need occur before Jesus returns; it teaches, rather, that such has been the case from the day of His ascension. Also called "any momentism."

Mid-tribulational rapturism: The idea that Jesus will take the saved from the earth at some point toward the middle of the seven-year tribulation period. Sometimes the view is associated with "partial rapturism," which sees only those who are especially prepared as being taken from the earth before the end of the tribulation while the remainder of Christians stay on earth and experience the tribulation, thus, a "mid-tribulational partial rapture."

Millennium: A word which derives from two Latin words ("mille" which means "thousand" and "annus" which means "year") that means "a thousand years" and refers to Jesus' coming reign on earth during such a time. (See Revelation 20:4–6)

Post-millennialism: The belief that, due to the positive effect of the preaching of the gospel, Christ's millennial reign will be brought about *after* which (thus *post*-millennial) Jesus will return.

Post-tribulationalism: The view that Jesus will return after the tribulation period or, put another way, that the Church will experience the tribulation period and not be taken out of the earth seven years earlier. It is not to be confused with post-millennialism.

Pre-millennialism: The doctrine that Jesus will return *before* the millennium (thus, *pre*-millennialism) to personally inaugurate His millennial kingdom. This doctrine is the explicit position of the early Church.

Pre-tribulationalism: The teaching that Jesus will take the Church away from the earth (usually seen as occurring seven years) before the tribulation begins. Also called "dispensational pre-tribulationalism" due to the dispensational frame-work into which the teaching is cast. The two things—pre-millennialism and pre-tribulationalism—often go together but must not be confused. Pre-millennialism was the common doctrine of the early church and was taught for over eighteen hundred years before the pre-tribulational rapture idea was ever taught. Put another way: one can be a pre-millennialist without any reference to pre-tribulationism. (See "historic" pre-millennialism.)

Pre-wrath rapture: In recent years some have begun teaching that Jesus will come after most of the seven-year tribulation period is over but before the wrath of God is poured out on the earth; therefore, the Church will experience most of the tribulation period while yet on earth.

Progressive dispensationalism: A rather new movement which does not see a total distinction between Israel and the Church—a position required by classic dispensationalism. Its adherents see the Church not as a "parenthesis" between Daniel's sixty-ninth and seventieth week. (Pre-tribulational dispensationalism teaches that God dealt essentially with the Jews in the first sixty-nine weeks, is dealing with the Church during the break between the sixty-ninth and seventieth week, and will begin dealing, essentially, with Israel and not the Church during the seventieth week.) God, then, according to this view, does not have two distinct purposes for His two peoples, Israel and the Church, but one. Progressive dispensationalism does, however, hold that God has a special purpose for Israel during the millennium during which time various Old Testament prophecies relating to Israel, including but not limited to the Jews' salvation (upon their belief in Christ) will be fulfilled.

Rapture: A word that refers to the specific aspect of Christ's Second Coming in which believers will be caught up from the earth. The word, not used in English translations of the New Testament, is from a Latin word *rapio* and means the same as the Greek word *harpadzo,* i.e., to snatch, to seize, to take away by force. Pre-tribulationalists teach that the event occurs seven years before Jesus' return to the earth. Post-tribulationalists say it occurs as one aspect of the Second Coming and that those caught up will immediately return to the earth with Christ at which time He will inaugurate His millennial rule.

Endnotes

Introduction and Part One

1. Jamiesson, Fausset, and Brown, editors, *Commentary, Practical and Explanatory on the Whole Bible* (Grand Rapids: Zondervan Publishing House, 1961), 866.

2. Robert Clouse, ed., *The Meaning of the Millennium* (Downer's Grove, IL: Intervarsity Press, 1977), 9.

3. G. E. Ladd, *Crucial Questions About the Kingdom of God* (Grand Rapids: William B. Eerdmans Publishing Company, 1956), 158.

4. Ed Hinson, "The Magi, the Madman and the Messiah," *National Liberty Journal* (December 2001), 11.

5. G. E. Ladd, *The Blessed Hope* (Grand Rapids: Willliam B. Eerdmans Publishing Company, 1956), 8.

6. C. I. Scofield, *Rightly Dividing the Word of Truth* (Neptune, NJ: Loizeaux Brothers, 1896).

7. Dave MacPherson, *The Rapture Plot* (Simpsonville, SC: Millennium III Publishers, 1995), 136.

8. Erwin Falhbusch, Jan Lochman, John Mbiti, Jaroslav Pelikan, Lukas Vischer, *The Encyclopedia of Christianity* (Grand Rapids: William B. Eerdmans Publishing Company, 1999), 854.

9. Robert Gundry, *The Church and the Tribulation* (Grand Rapids: Zondervan Publishing House, 1973), 175.

10. Ibid, 175.

11. Van Kampen, *The Sign* (Wheaton, IL: Crossway Books, 1992), 449f; G.E. Ladd, *The Blessed Hope* (Grand Rapids: William B. Eerdmans Publishing Company, 1956), 19f; Robert Gundry, *The Church and the Tribulation* (Grand Rapids: Zondervan Publishing Company, 1973), 172f; Gundry, *First the Antichrist* (Grand Rapids: Baker Books, 1997), 143f; Dave MacPherson, *The Great Rapture Hoax* (Fletcher, NC: New Puritan Library Publishers, 1983), 16f; Alexander Reese, *The Approaching Advent of Christ* (Grand Rapids: Grand Rapids International Publications, 1975), 18.

12. H.C. Thiessen, *Lectures in Systematic Theology* (Grand Rapids: William B. Eerdmans Publishing Company, 1936), 370f.

13. Gundry, *The Church and the Tribulation,* 172–173.

14. John Walvoord, *The Rapture Question* (Grand Rapids: Academie Books, 1979), 156–157.

Part Two

1. Warren Wiersbe, *The Bible Exposition Commentary,* Vol. 2 (Colorado Springs: Chariot Victor Publishing Company, 1989), 581–582.

2. John Walvoord, *The Rapture Question* (Grand Rapids: Academie Books, 1979), 34–35.

3. William Rowlands, *Our Lord Cometh* (London: Sovereign Grace Advent Testimony, 1930), 62–63.

4. John F. Walvoord, *The Rapture Question* (Findlay, OH: Dunham Publishing Company, 1957), 246.

5. Robert Gundry, *The Church and the Tribulation* (Grand Rapids: Zondervan Publishing House, 1973), 104.

6. Arthur Katterjohn, *The Tribulation People* (Carol Stream, IL: Creation House, 1975), 44.

7. C.I. Scofield, E. Schuyler English, Frank E. Gabelein, William Culbertson, et al. *The New Scofield Reference Bible* (New York: Oxford University Press, 1967), 1250.

8. Walvoord, *Rapture Question,* 170.

9. Ibid, 171.

10. Ibid, 246.

11. Tim Lahaye, *Revelation* (Grand Rapids: Zondervan Publishing House, 1976), 75–76.

12. Scofield, *The New Scofield Reference Bible,* 1356.

13. Walvoord, *Rapture Question,* 258–259.

14. Jerry Falwell, *Liberty Bible Commentary* (Lynchburg, VA: The Old-time Gospel Hour, 1982), 802–803.

15. Scofield, *New Scofield Bible,* 135b.

16. Henry C. Theissen, *Lectures in Systematic Theology,* (Grand Rapids: William B. Eerdmans Publishing Company, 1949), 379.

17. Alexander Reese, *The Approaching Advent of Christ* (Grand Rapids: Grand Rapids International Publications, 1975), 94.

18. Robert Gundry, *The Church and the Tribulation* (Grand Rapids: Zondervan Publishing House, 1973), 55f.

19. C.I. Scofield, *Addresses on Prophecy* (Greenville, SC: The Gospel Hour, Inc.), 99.

20. Walvoord, *Rapture Question,* 258–259.

21. Reese, *The Approaching Advent of Christ,* 125–183.

22. Gundry, *The Church and the Tribulation,* 115.

23. E. Schuyler English, *Re-thinking the Rapture* (Travelers Rest, SC: Southern Bible Book House, 1954), 67.

24. Ibid, 69.

25. Ibid, 69.

26. Charles C. Ryrie, *The Ryrie Study Bible,* (Chicago: Moody Press, 1995), 374.

27. Walvoord, *Rapture Question,* 68–69.

28. John F. Walvoord, *The Rapture Question Revised and Enlarged Edition* (Grand Rapids: Academie Books, 1979), 258.

29. George E. Ladd, *The Blessed Hope* (Grand Rapids: William B. Eerdmans Publishing Company, 1956), 150–151.

30. Robert Gundry, *First the Antichrist* (Grand Rapids: Baker Books, 1997), 56.

31. Reese, *The Approaching Advent of Christ,* 215.

Part Three

1. John F. Walvoord, *The Rapture Question* (Findlay, OH: Dunham Publishing Company, 1957), 181.

2. Ibid, 182.

3. Robert Gundry, *First the Antichrist* (Grand Rapids: Baker Books, 1997), 146.

4. Dave MacPherson, *The Great Rapture Hoax* (Fletcher, NC: New Puritan Library Publishers, 1983), 19.

5. A.H. Strong, *Systematic Theology* (Philadelphia: The Judson Press, 1907), 1006.

6. James White, *The Forgotten Trinity* (Minneapolis: Bethany House Publishers, 1998), 178f.

7. John F. Walvoord, *The Rapture Question* (Findlay, OH: Dunham Publishing Company, 1957), 51, 73, and 75.

8. Ibid, 216–219.

9. C.I. Scofield, E. Schuyler English, Frank E. Gabelein, William Culbertson, et al. *The New Scofield Reference Bible* (New York: Oxford University Press, 1967), 1353.

10. G. E. Ladd, *The Blessed Hope* (Grand Rapids: Willliam B. Eerdmans Publishing Company, 1956), 151.

11. Theodor Storm, "Pastor Niemoller and His Creed," translated by Margaret Blount (London: Hodder and Stoughton, 1939), 42.

12. Philip Jenkins, *The Next Christendom* (New York: Oxford University Press, 2002), 216–219.

13. Dave MacPherson, *The Three R's: Rapture, Revisionism, and Robbery* (Simpsonville, SC: P.O.S.T. Publishers, 1998), 9.

14. Ibid, 9.

15. John F. Walvoord, *The Rapture Question* (Findlay, OH: Dunham Publishing Company, 1957), 64.

16. Charles C. Ryrie, *Dispensationalism Today* (Chicago: Moody Press, 1965), 159–160.

17. J.W. Pentecost, *Things to Come* (Grand Rapids: Zondervan Publishing House, 1958), 121.

18. Ibid, 122.

19. Ibid, 123.

20. Ibid, 122.

21. Ibid, 124.

22. William E. Bell, *A Critical Evaluation of the Pretribulation Rapture Doctrine in Christian Theology* (Ph.D. diss., New York University, 1967), 124.

23. Ibid, 189.

24. Bell, *A Critical Evaluation of the Pretribulation Rapture Doctrine in Christian Theology,* 16.

25. Walvoord, *Rapture Question,* 217.

26. Bernard Ramm, *Protestant Biblical Interpretation: A Textbook of Hermeneutics for Conservative Protestants* (Boston: W.A. Wilde Company, 1956), 245.

27. Hal Lindsey, *The Late Great Planet Earth* (Grand Rapids: Zondervan Publishing Company, 1970), 131.

28. As to the supposed incompatibilities between Jesus' and Paul's eschatology, let the interested student peruse—to mention a few excellent sources—Theodore Zahn's introductory materials to the Thessalonian letters in his "Introduction to the New Testament," Vol. l, translated by J.M. Trout, et al (Edingburgh: T. and T. Clark, 1909), 223–224; Norman Douty, *The Great Tribulation Debate* (Harrison, AR: Gibbs Publishing Company, 1956), 44f; Gleason Archer, Paul Feinberg, Douglas Moo, and Richard Reiter, *The Rapture: Pre,-Mid,-or Post-Tribulational* (Grand Rapids: Academie Books, 1984), 194 and 206; and especially Alexander Reese's meticulous cataloguing of the comparison of the eschatological teachings of Jesus and Paul in his *The Approaching Advent of Christ* (Grand Rapids: Grand Rapids International Publications, 1975), 259–261, in all of which places the compatibility is clearly demonstrated. An excellent survey appears in the aforementioned unpublished doctoral thesis by William E. Bell, 249–250.

29. Bell, *A Critical Evaluation of the Pretribulation Rapture Doctrine in Christian Theology,* 250.

30. Ibid, 248–249.

31. Ibid, 359.

32. Betty Padice, ed. *Early Christian Writings* (London: Penguin Books, 1968), 187f.

33. *Ryrie Study Bible,* Expanded Edition, Moody Press, 1195, 2034.

34. Paul Enns, *The Moody Handbook of Prophecy* (Chicago: Moody Press, 1989), 633.

35. Ladd, *The Blessed Hope,* 93–94.

36. Robert Gundry, *First the Antichrist* (Grand Rapids: Baker Books, 1997), 41–42.

37. Reese, *The Approaching Advent of Christ* (Grand Rapids: Grand Rapids International Publications), 180–181.

38. Roland Rasmussen, *The Post-trib, Pre-wrath Rapture* (Canoga Park, CA: The Post-trib Research Center, 1996).

39. Southern Baptist Convention, *The Baptist Faith and Message* (Nashville: LifeWay Christian Resources, 2000), 15.

40. MacPherson, *The Great Rapture Hoax,* 24–25.

41. Ibid, 86.

Part Four

1. J.W.C. Wand, *The Four Great Heresies* (London: A.R. Mowbray & Company, 1955), 15.

2. J.W. Dwight Pentecost, *Things to Come* (Grand Rapids: Zondervan Publishing House, 1958), 203 and 392–393.

3. Ibid, 203.

4. John F. Walvoord, *The Rapture Question Revised and Enlarged Edition* (Grand Rapids: Academie Books, 1979), 253.

5. Ibid, 13–14.

6. John F. Walvoord, *The Revelation of Jesus Christ* (Chicago: Moody, Press, 1966),103.

7. Ibid, 103.

8. William E. Bell, *A Critical Evaluation of the Pretribulation Rapture Doctrine in Christian Theology* (Ph.D. diss., New York University, 1967), 317.

9. John F. Walvoord, *The Rapture Question* (Findlay, OH: Dunham Publishing Company, 1957), 186.

10. Ibid, 140.

11. Ibid, 186.

12. Charles C. Ryrie, *Dispensationalism Today* (Chicago: Moody Press, 1965), 159–160.

13. Bell, *A Critical Evaluation of the Pretribulation Rapture Doctrine in Christian Theology,* 352.

14. Alexander Reese, *The Approaching Advent of Christ* (Grand Rapids: Grand Rapids International Publications, 1975), 244.

Part Five

1. Billy Graham, *Till Armageddon* (Waco, TX: Word Books, 1981), 8.

2. Don Moen, "God Will Make a Way," Integrity Hosanna Music, ©1990.

3. Roger G. Branch and Larry A. Platt, Resources for Ministry in Death and Dying (Nashville: Broadman Holman, 1988), 119.

4. Walter Kaiser, *Hard Sayings of the Bible* (Downers Grove, IL: Intervarsity Press, 1996), 720.

5. Philip Jenkins, *The Next Christendom* (New York: Oxford University Press, 2002), 218.

Bibliography

Bell, William E. "A Critical Evaluation of the Pretribulation Rapture Doctrine in Christian Theology." Ph.D diss., New York University, New York, 1967.

Biederwolf, William E. *The Millennium Bible*. Grand Rapids: Baker Book House, 1964.

Burton, Dewitt B., and Stevens, William A. *Harmony of the Gospels*. New York: Charles Scribner's Sons, 1893.

Clouse, Robert, ed. *The Meaning of the Millennium*. Downer's Grove, Illinois, 1977.

Douty, Norman F. *Has Christ's Return Two Stages?* New York: Pageant Press, Inc., 1956.

————. *The Great Tribulation Debate*. Harrison, Arkansas: Gibbs Publishing Company, 1976.

English, E. Schuyler. *Re-thinking The Rapture*. Travelers Rest, South Carolina: Southern Bible Book House, 1954.

Enns, Paul. *The Moody Handbook of Theology*. Chicago: Moody Press, 1989.

Falwell, Jerry, ed., *Liberty Bible Commentary*. Nashville: Thomas Nelson, 1982.

Fuller, Daniel P. "The Hermeneutics of Dispensationalism." PH.D. diss., Northern Baptist Theological Seminary, Chicago, Illinois, 1957.

Gundry, Robert. *The Church and the Tribulation*. Grand Rapids: Zondervan, 1973.

―――. *First The Antichrist*. Grand Rapids: Baker Books, 1997.

Jenkins, Philip. *The Next Christendom*. New York: Oxford, 2002.

Katterjohn, Arthur. *The Tribulation People*. Carol Stream, Illinois: Creation House Publishers, 1975.

Ladd, George E. *The Blessed Hope*. Grand Rapids: William B. Eerdmans Publishing Company, 1956.

―――. *Commentary on the Revelation of John*. Grand Rapids: William B. Eerdmans Publishing Company, 1972.

―――. *The Last Things*. Grand Rapids: William B. Eerdmans Publishing Company, 1978.

LaHaye, Tim. *Revelation*. Grand Rapids: Zondervan, 1975.

LaSor, William S. *The Truth About Armageddon*. Grand Rapids: Baker Book House, 1982.

Lindsey, Hal. *The Late Great Planet Earth*. Grand Rapids: Zondervan, 1970.

Lindsell, Harold. *The Gathering Storm*. Wheaton, Illinois: Tyndale House Publishers, 1980.

MacPherson, Dave. *The Great Rapture Hoax*. Fletcher, NC: New Puritan Library Publishers, 1983.

―――. *The Incredible Cover-up*. Plainfield, New Jersey: Logos International, 1975.

―――. *The Rapture Plot*. Simpsonville, SC: Millennium III Publishers, 1995.

―――. *The Three R's*. Simpsonville, SC: P.O.S.T Publishers, 1998.

————. *The Unbelievable Pre-trib Origin*. Kansas City: Heart of America Bible Society Publishers, 1973.

Payne, J. Barton. *Encyclopedia of Biblical Prophecy*. New York: Harper and Row, 1973.

Pentecost, J. Dwight. *Things To Come*. Grand Rapids: Zondervan, 1958.

Rasmussen, Roland. *The Post-trib, Pre-wrath Rapture*. Canoga Park, California: The Post-Trib Research Center, 1996.

Reese, Alexander. *The Approaching Advent of Christ*. Grand Rapids: Grand Rapids International Publications, 1975.

Reiter, Richard R, Gleason Archer, Paul D. Feinberg, and Douglas Moo. *The Rapture*. Grand Rapids: Academie, 1984.

Robertson, A. T. *A Harmony of the Gospels*. New York: Harper & Row, Publishers, 1922.

Rowlands, William J. *Our Lord Cometh*. London: The Sovereign Grace Advent Testimony, 1964.

Ryrie, Charles C. *Dispensationalism Today*. Chicago: Moody Press, 1965.

Stanton, Gerald B. *Kept From the Hour*. Miami Springs, Florida: Schoettel Publishing Company, Inc., 1991.

Thiessen, Henry C. *Lectures in Systematic Theology*. Grand Rapids: William B. Eerdmans Publishing Company, 1949.

Tregelles, S. P. *The Hope of Christ's Second Coming*. London: The Sovereign Grace Advent Testimony, 1864.

Walvoord, John F. *The Rapture Question*. Findlay, Ohio: Dunham Publishing Company, 1957.

————. *The Rapture Question: Revised and Enlarged Edition*. Grand Rapids: Academie Books, 1979.

————. *The Revelation*. Chicago, Illinois: Moody Press, 1966.

About the Author

Dr. William E. Anderson is a graduate of Baylor University and Southwestern Baptist Theological Seminary. He recently retired from Calvary Baptist Church in Clearwater, Florida, where he served as senior pastor for twenty-seven years. He currently resides in Clearwater, Florida, with his wife of forty-seven years. He enjoys filling his time with writing, speaking engagements, and spending time with his fifteen grandchildren.